INDUSTRIAL TRAINING SYSTEMS AND RECORDS

Industrial Training Systems and Records

GERARD TAVERNIER

Gower Press

First published in Britain by Gower Press Limited
140 Great Portland Street, London W1N 5TA
1971

© Gower Press Limited, 1971
ISBN 0 7161 0084 3

Set in 11 on 13 point Times and printed and bound in Britain by
R. J. Acford Ltd , Industrial Estate, Chichester, Sussex

Contents

Illustrations

Acknowledgements

For their advice and assistance and their permission to study their procedures, I am grateful and indebted to the following companies:

Bentalls Limited, Kingston-upon-Thames

British Aircraft Corporation, Weybridge

Colt International, Havant

Corah Limited, Leicester

The Dowty Group, Cheltenham

The General Post Office

The Joseph Lucas Group, Birmingham

The National Coal Board

Rolls-Royce Aero-Engine Division, Derby

Trocoll Ideal Services Group

Grateful acknowledgement is also made to the staff of *Personnel Management*, journal of the Institute of Personnel Management, and Industrial Trainers for their cooperation, as well as to the various industrial training boards, whose published recommendations proved useful, and to suppliers of forms and records, in particular Kalamazoo Limited and Shannon Limited.

G Tavernier

Publisher's Note

The illustrative material in this book is drawn from actual documents used by a variety of companies, to whom acknowledgements are expressed on the opposite page.

The need for a standard format in book reproduction means that the size and proportions of many documents have had to be modified in the following pages. The essential information carried by each form, however, remains unaltered.

For similar reasons of rationalisation, the mechanical data carried at the top of forms has also been omitted. Such data includes:

1   Company name or letterhead, address, telephone and telegraphic details

2   Company logo or emblem

3   Actual reference numbers and dates

Firms using this book to design or adapt their own recording systems will, of course, draw up forms of a shape and size to suit their own requirements, adding the appropriate data listed above.

The information entered on some forms is intended to suggest how the forms are completed and is fictitious.

1

Training Administration

Whatever the size or type of operation, effective training requires first a detailed analysis of training requirements. The subsequent evaluation of training methods, and appraisal of performance and potential imply the maintenance and *use* of accurate and comprehensive records in order that training efforts be developed and controlled in the most economical and effective way. High priority should be given to the periodic analysis of training records and systems in the light of changing conditions.

In large organisations training may be able to call on O & M, work study, systems analysis or other management services to look into problems and develop administrative systems. These advisory services have two main advantages over do-it-yourself method study. Firstly, they can put someone on the investigation full time, without interrupting him continually to cope with urgent short-term jobs. Secondly, they have made a special study of how to investigate and improve methods. But it is necessary for the training staff to provide the knowledge on what is being done as well as the objectives.

Any form or procedure which has been in use without alteration for some time is a target for re-examination. Circumstances change all the time, and it often happens that reports continue to be prepared or forms procured or procedures followed even though they have become unsuitable or unnecessary. Forms often increase in number and procedures tend to get more complicated as time goes on, and any new procedure should attempt to integrate all those haphazardly devised forms raised to meet specific purposes. A lot more could be done, too, to integrate records held by personnel and training. Occasional ruthless audits into the value of the information to those who receive it, compared with the cost of providing it, can lead to surprising simplifications. Success does not require an entire revolution of existing methods; a single change where most needed can pay off handsomely.

The introduction of training records on computer will undoubtedly provide an opportunity to take a fresh look at the whole purpose of a procedure, what is actually being done and what could and should be done, instead of simply making the minimum changes required for computer compatability.

CRITERIA FOR AN EFFECTIVE INFORMATION SYSTEM

To be effective an information system should possess at least the following characteristics:

1   It should be simple
2   It should be relevant to the purpose of training, and the records sought and the information derived from them should be relevant to the company and to training objectives
3   The information produced should be of the depth and scope needed
4   It should provide a means of obtaining information and dissemination of information with a minimum of paper and clerical work
5   The required information should be distributed regularly and promptly to ensure quick action and attention to problems
6   It should concentrate on those areas which most demand attention
7   And, finally, a good system should be planned for expansion and possible introduction on computer

Standard definitions and standard methods are necessary, particularly when comparisons are made between factories or departments or between different intakes. Varying methods of calculation arising from different interpretations give rise to different figures; numbers being trained may or may not include those training on the job, for example, and this should be made clear.

A manual should be provided to those responsible for supplying information to ensure that procedures are followed and that the documents are submitted as required.

LINES OF RESPONSIBILITY

The organisation of the training function and its lines of responsibility depend very much on the size, the nature and the *modus operandi* of the enterprise, and the training services provided. Ideally it should be responsible directly to the board. In a large number of firms, training is linked with personnel, particularly where training does not have the responsibility for management development. It is significant, however, that a number of progressive firms have transferred the responsibility for training to industrial relations, with all that that implies, or to manpower planning, so that the training activities can be based on *future* organisation and *future* needs.

It is also important that the training activities themselves be decentralised, with substantial autonomy, controlled centrally only through operating budgets, reviews of performance and training policies and objectives. Training is not an activity that can be *administered* and the training function itself should not become the focal point to refer all problems and grievances. Nor should it remain on the periphery; training is an intrinsic part of the enterprise and its activities should be expected to contribute to increased productivity and greater profitability. This means that the training staff must be very much involved in day-to-day operations so that they may remain pragmatic in their approach and react more quickly to changes.

Training organisation at the Perkins Engines Group provides a good example of how the training function can be largely integrated into the company structure without interfering with line management. To some extent the approach adopted in other areas of management, such as finance, is used by training. An "employee resourcing manager," responsible for recruitment, training and management development, and salary administration, is assigned to each production area. This concept integrates personnel and training activities and in effect places in each production area a senior personnel manager who can rely on the employee resourcing services department to perform most of the administrative work. The basic work in manpower planning and management development is carried out by the divisional resourcing managers, but coordination of these activities is managed centrally to avoid obvious anomalies in training policies and performance appraisals, for example, not to mention salary administration and industrial relations.

The resourcing services department provides the basic training courses to teach common skills and control activities, while the divisional resourcing managers are responsible for meeting specialised on-the-job training requirements. This is because the company accepts the belief that the role and needs of supervisors, for example, vary widely in different parts of the same company. In operator training, the twenty-five instructors report to the line managers, not to the resourcing managers who have only functional responsibilities. It is their duty, however, to identify training needs, ensure that the instructors know the latest training techniques, assist in selection and training of instructors and ensure that the training board requirements are met.

TRAINING COMMITTEES

Training committees are useful in involving senior management and obtaining their commitment to training, particularly when training is being introduced formally and systematically for the first time. Once a training policy and objectives have been agreed and training programmes established, it is doubtful whether such committees remain effective. Members are often remote from the training situation and lack the necessary understanding of job skills to be able to discuss training techniques properly.

Training committees prove useful in controlling training activities and ensuring that policy is being implemented uniformly in large organisations with enterprises dispersed throughout the country.

The National Coal Board for example has a standing training committee composed of area representatives, the Industrial Training Branch at the NCB headquarters and the headquarters computer services situated at Cannock, Staffordshire. The statistics department and headquarters manpower branch are consulted as necessary. This committee assists in the planning and control of training and is responsible for reviewing and determining the additional information needed by training branches at unit, area and headquarters level and for ensuring that information on the EDP system is efficiently produced.

Committees concerned with specific training schemes can sometimes be useful, particularly when trainees are dispersed throughout the company. The National Coal Board, for example, has a joint advisory committee which meets twice yearly to discuss clerical and commercial training. Within the Joseph Lucas Organisation in Birmingham there are several committees concerned specifically with management development. The committee in each company meets monthly and generally comprises the general manager, the production engineer, director of engineering, the purchasing and sales managers and the executive development officer. Joseph Lucas also have an advisory committee for apprenticeship training which meets every three months. These meetings are chaired by an executive director from one of the companies, the director of production engineering, the apprenticeship training manager, the tool room manager and an engineering designer. The group training manager attends to record decisions to be implemented but does not participate in the discussions.

Ad hoc committees are sometimes set up to discuss improvements or problems as the need arises, and then dissolved once the necessary decisions have been made for the training function to carry out. The British Aircraft Corporation set up committees to introduce metrication and decimalisation, for instance. Rolls-Royce, for example, early in 1968 formed a working party comprising divisional and senior managers from major operations to improve training arrangements for post-graduates. As a result Rolls-Royce has been able to reduce the length of apprenticeship for several important groups of graduates, enabling them to be placed into jobs that much sooner. Only induction and specialised training are now given on initial appointment and further education and training are dealt with at later stages as needs are diagnosed through standard career development programmes. Another major group of graduates, incidentally, particularly in mechanical engineering but also including scientists, mathematicians and a few economists, join Rolls-Royce as undergraduate apprentices for a year or six months before going to university, later returning for a year's post-graduate training.

It often happens that a committee may be formed, not necessarily to discuss training, but other problems which may be of concern to the training function, which should therefore be represented. Such committees have been formed to meet problems arising out of metrication and decimalisation, for example, or to rationalise and reduce paperwork. The National Coal Board has a standing committee, comprising of representatives of the medical services, production and industrial relations, among others, responsible for maintaining an efficient medical service and covering first aid training.

UNION REPRESENTATION

The Industrial Training Act has had a great effect on industrial relations as yet un-realised by employers, who generally still consider it their prerogative to train whom they please how they please without soliciting union agreement. It seems inevitable however that unions will demand a greater say in training at company level. Until now, interest was primarily in the number of apprentices taken on, particularly in areas with long histories of unemployment, and the protection of the seniority and security of existing employees. Since the introduction of the modular system in the engineering industry, however, there has been growing interest in the assessment of apprentices at the end of each module and the standards of work established to determine whether or not a trainee is qualified. As higher rates of pay are based on the attainment of a degree of skills, conflict could conceivably develop over the assessment between the supervisors and instructors on the one hand and union officials who may question a trainee's competence on the other. It has also yet to be resolved whether or not a trainee who completes a third or a fourth module is entitled to more pay than another who has begun working after completing a second.

While it is true that trade unions are represented on the Central Training Council and on the various industrial training boards, it is at the workplace that union consent must be obtained. Trade unionists are however by no means opposed to training, but are interested chiefly in protecting the welfare of their members. There should be few problems if employers can show evidence of proper manpower planning, adequate redundancy procedures, including provisions for retraining, compensation and social security, and realistic bargaining about sharing gains in productivity at the point of production.

It would also seem feasible to seek at least union consent to standards of training being established and reduction of apprenticeship time and, as a matter of courtesy, to explain changes in training arrangements and syllabus. Any industrial relations problems arising out of training should not be handled by training but referred to senior management and industrial relations. But it is training's responsibility to anticipate industrial relations problems arising out of proposed changes in training policy or arrangements and to inform senior management of them.

TRAINING OBJECTIVES

For training to be relevant and effective, it is essential for management to be able to establish priorities and the resources required. This requires first the establishment of training objectives and a clear statement from management on how these are to be achieved.

Objectives can be established only after considerable thought and analysis; this in fact may be the most valuable part of the exercise. The amalgam of objectives will be different for each individual company.

The first essential of any training policy is that it be directly linked to the company objectives, taking into consideration technological developments and market changes. Training objectives within the Joseph Lucas Organisation, for example, are firmly established as an integral part of the company's operations improvement programme on which are based departmental objectives, product group objectives and company objectives. From these the company can assess the requirements: new techniques, improved control information, changes in organisation structures and the consequently changing needs of individuals. And training needs are based on these.

When the recommendations of an industrial training board are applicable they should of course be considered. However, board grants are based on an assessment of an industry's needs and under no circumstances should a firm's training activities be dictated by grants. In any event, the size of grant cannot be accurately forecast, particularly where boards use vague "adjustment" or "weighting" factors, even where their recommendations are followed closely. Cost analysis may show that the expense of following a board's recommendations can be more than the grant it is prepared to pay. One must also consider the time consumed in form filling and record keeping to claim grants and interruption in manufacturing, for example.

POLICY STATEMENT

To be useful, a statement of policy must go beyond stating general aspirations and make clear to management at all levels and in all functions the company's intention and how it is to be carried out.

It is essential, of course, that any policy regarding training be in harmony with the company's personnel policies on recruitment, salaries, promotion and security of employment, for example, and be integrated with the company's overall objectives. It should indicate any differences in general conditions of employment for trainees; the National Coal Board allows apprentices seven "rest days" in addition to the regular holidays given other employees, for example.

A Training Policy is normally affected by the following considerations:

Market development
Technological development
Social development
External situation
Company commercial objectives as determined by the board of directors' resources, capital and plant, material and design, labour and initiative
Company plans covering management, finance, plant, material and personnel
Organisation and manpower plans
Operating policies

Efforts should be made to avoid vague and obscure statements and, while policy must be specific in principle, it must avoid minute details of *how* it is to be carried out. At the same time, it must have a sense of permanence and yet remain flexible.

In addition, the training function should establish standing operating procedures for the following:

1   Recruitment and selection of trainees
2   Retraining
3   Post-experience training
4   Further education (day or block release)
5   Prerequisites for acceptance in training schemes
6   Hours of training
7   Physical examinations
8   Aptitude and personality tests
9   Pay while in training
10 Lodging allowance
11 Travel grants
12 Duration of training
13 Probationary periods
14 Qualifications for entering particular departments or jobs
15 Timekeeping and method of reporting
16 Wage increases
17 Absences
18 Responsibility for obtaining required tools and equipment
19 Damage to, or loss of, company property
20 Accident prevention, liability and notification
21 Discipline (drinking, gambling, etc)
22 Parking
23 Status of trainee, and procedure for recognition as regular employee
24 Payment of fees for attending or completing a course satisfactorily
25 Authority to attend external courses

REPORTS TO MANAGEMENT

Senior management need to be kept informed of training developments and changing training requirements to meet company objectives. A records system should be so designed as to provide the required information easily; data collated hurriedly is often unreliable and therefore worthless.

Data on training is usually requested on a regular basis, monthly, quarterly or annually, and is often included as part of a larger report covering personnel, labour relations or manpower planning generally.

Some companies require certain information on costs or available manpower monthly or quarterly, and all other information annually. When submitting figures for an annual report, the opportunity should be taken to discuss future training needs and objectives and any obstacles requiring the attention of top management.

Reports to management could include such information as:

1   Numbers trained (by category and overall)
2   Jobs they were trained for
3   Numbers of trainees lost
4   Changes in training schemes
5   New training standards
6   New courses being developed
7   Methods of dealing with expansion plans

TRAINING BUDGETS

The recognised importance of training in the past few years has led to a tendency to give free rein to training functions to purchase whatever is necessary for their operations. Employers want the training staff to feel free to ask for what they need, but lack of a budget in fact inhibit instructors from making requests for fear of "overdoing it." Thus, more reserved instructors are impeded by lack of proper facilities or effective training aids.

It is argued that a budget is limiting; but that of course is the whole point of budgeting. Budgetary control is necessary to ensure that resources are allocated to various training schemes according to priority, and generally ensuring that training is achieved with economy and purpose. With reliable cost data it is possible to judge whether a given type of training is proving beneficial. Reliable figures help to justify the cost of training operations in terms of benefits and thus help to obtain the necessary funds for further development when necessary. Perhaps more important, with a budget, training can be considered in relation to other company needs and be given the priority it deserves. It ensures that training is carried out progressively and not on a stop-go basis from year to year.

The industrial training boards are not concerned with training costs as long as they are convinced that they are being determined in an accepted manner. Generally the boards are content with statistically determined costs. The only cost a board can audit by law is the payroll for the year in order to calculate the levy.

Training should be costed and budgeted as any other activity. The training budget should conform to the company's accounting system, although there are those who believe that, if necessary, existing budgeting formats should be modified to accommodate training since training costs are after all fairly substantial, even if only a levy is paid. It is useful, for example, to have the training budget conform to the same fiscal period as that covered by the industry's training board. Many firms, however, keep levy and grant separate from the training budget. The levy is charged to total operating costs of the enterprise or as a direct labour cost, like National Insurance or SET, and grant is considered company profit. In this way training is dissuaded from trying to recoup the levy as such or aim for grant maximisation. One firm charged its initial levy in the first year to operations and applies the grant return each year to the following year's levy, so that only the difference need to be accounted for.

Basically there are two methods of allocating training budgets; both have the same result but the method used may greatly influence decision making. Using the first method, all training costs are absorbed by training, using the same coding system as is used in every other department. This system has the advantage that all training costs are recorded in one place and, perhaps more important, that control of trainees and selection of external courses in training are not left with individual managers. It also indicates to others that training is controlled and its activities must be justified in the same way as any other function.

The other method is to assign all costs of training to the regular departmental budgets. In this way, expenditure must be authorised and be controlled by individual line managers, including off-the-job training centres. This method makes the line manager more conscious of training and the need to relate it to departmental performance. The main disadvantage is the loss of control by training over expenditure and in establishing priorities.

CAPITAL EXPENDITURE

Capital expenditure requires tight control and this is normally authorised on an appropriation release form which must be approved by a special committee or at various levels of management. Capital expenditure proposals are often made on a capital budget made annually. Once this has received board approval, standard requisitions can then be prepared by training as they need specific items.

Details of budgeting and cost analysis are beyond the scope of this book. However, to be effective, a training budget must be based on anticipated training needs and not simply on the previous year's expenditure, with an added percentage which in any case management normally cuts.

2

Identifying Training Needs

In order to be able to establish training objectives it is necessary to determine the training required to provide the skills, knowledge and attitudes for meeting company objectives. There are many uncertainties in carrying out this kind of forecasting, which make it all the more important that any identification of future training needs to be systematic and comprehensive.

The identification of training needs requires a careful use of manpower planning reports. Manpower planning is largely concerned with the number and type of employees and the skills required on a long-range basis, taking into consideration such factors as wastage, retraining plans, retirements and deaths. Manpower planning reports should, therefore, be carefully scrutinised by training and the method of calculation and dependability of figures questioned. If necessary the format of manpower planning reports and the way in which the figures are presented should be altered to complement training records.

Figure 2:1 shows a form of management manpower plan which has been recommended by several industrial training boards for medium-sized firms. In larger firms it may be advantageous to subdivide the jobs according to category (technological, sales, engineering, and so on) and to elaborate on the table.

It is essential to assemble all relevant internal information and supplement this whenever necessary with interviews and personal observation. Reports may need to be adapted or expanded for the training function's use; in fact, the format of departmental reports should be altered if necessary to provide the information required by training. The following list, although not comprehensive, may suggest some of the sources of information in identifying training needs:

1   Accident reports
2   Reports on labour turnover, absenteeism, etc
3   Consultant studies
4   Management services reports

5   Quality control records
6   Attitude surveys
7   Salary surveys
8   Amendments to procedures manuals
9   Industrial relations reports on disputes containing grievances raised in arbitration
10   Adverse probationary reports on new employees
11   Succession plans
12   Production figures
13   Reports arising from analyses of crises

The annual report is another good source of information as well as public speeches made by various managers to outside organisations. Copies of these can usually be obtained from the public relations office. Areas of weaknesses and the need for more advanced or different knowledge may emerge from discussions with course members, and instructions should be given to instructors to report these.

External factors should also be investigated by the training function. These would include such things as changes in government policies (metrication and decimalisation are good examples), marketing trends which could affect distribution, transportation and stock control. It is also essential to keep abreast of the latest developments in technology whose applications would involve radical changes in job content or work arrangements. These could include new management techniques as well as new processes. Such information can normally be obtained from trade and technical journals, textbooks, course prospectuses, newspapers, radio and television programmes, and from reports published by trade, professional and employers' associations, the industrial training boards, the HMSO, the Department of Employment and Productivity and such government agencies as the National Economic Development Office and the "little Neddies." It is also helpful to study national agreements and productivity agreements reached in other companies.

The number, type and quality of trainees are also affected by developments outside the company. Clearly, new industries moving into the area may affect the level of recruitment. Information on future labour availability and general trends likely to affect manpower supply can be obtained from the local offices of the DEP and the Youth Employment Office. Expansion or development plans for local technical colleges should also be scrutinised as this may affect decisions being made regarding in-company training facilities.

INDIVIDUAL TRAINING NEEDS

It is also essential to determine training needs on an individual basis, either to improve individual performance or prepare particular individuals for additional or higher responsibilities. By coding personal records it is possible to obtain regular lists of key and senior personnel scheduled to retire. The training function in the Joseph Lucas Organisation receive regular lists of impending promotions as well as retirements, and a report on changes being made in the managerial structure and of new positions being created. This report is issued monthly, even if only one name appears on it. After some time to give them a chance to settle in and become acquainted with their work, newly-appointed and promoted managers are visited by an executive development officer to discuss ways in which training could be of help in discharging their new tasks.

Measurement of performance will of course indicate individual training needs. One of the oldest and still most useful forms for establishing training needs of operators is the TWI chart designed by the Ministry of Labour, now the Department of Employment and Productivity. Figure 2:2, based on the TWI form, shows which operator needs training, of what kind, and how soon it should be achieved.

At management and supervisory levels, individual training needs can be identified through a more formal process of performance appraisal, involving a formal analysis of the skills and knowledge required and a comparison of the individual's performance with the objectives of the job agreed by himself in consultation with his immediate superior. A training programme is then prepared stating the type and depth of training required by the individual to perform his job effectively. In practice this is accomplished by preparing a job description, that is, a short list of the main tasks involved in the job, followed by a job specification, listing the skills, knowledge and attitude required, and the key results areas, that is where improvements would prove most beneficial. Objectives are then agreed and a training programme created to remedy any deficiencies in the individual in his ability to achieve the desired results. This procedure in itself is an important element in the training of managers, since it requires each one to monitor his own activities. It also involves line management in the training process by making them establish training needs, formulate training programmes and assess results. It also serves as a basis of career development through training and experience for junior managers who are being groomed for succession. For these reasons, the procedure is now recommended by virtually all the individual training boards.

JOB DESCRIPTIONS

The preparation of a job description requires a thorough analysis of the nature and extent of each of a manager's main tasks. A written statement is then prepared describing the main duties, responsibilities and requirements of the job. Vague job descriptions lead to equally vague training specifications, however. Terms such as "responsible for product quality" or "shared responsibility for safety" are of little help. The job description should be a statement of what these duties mean in terms of activities, and the results which the job exists to achieve, not the duties, responsibilities or activities he undertakes. For example, one of a production manager's main objectives would be to complete the products on time and the emphasis should be on that, rather than on, say, the techniques of production planning which are the means used to attain the objective.

By restricting the job description in this way, it is possible to discover whether or not more than one person is held responsible for the same decisions or whether decisions are being left to chance. It is also much easier to evaluate later whether or not the expected results have been achieved. It should not, however, be necessary to include all the responsibilities inherent in a job, but only those which are most important in terms of results.

Job description forms basically contain the following information:

1   The most appropriate title for the position
2   The main purpose of the position
3   The main duties
4   Lines of authority: the relationship with senior and subordinate managers and with other functions
5   The resources, human and financial
6   Limits of authority

Figure 2:3 is a typical example of a job description. Figure 2:3 is, in fact, the first page of a performance evaluation form which is described later.

JOB SPECIFICATIONS

Job descriptions are sometimes accompanied by a job specification which is essentially a statement interpreting the required skills, knowledge and attitude which a person must possess to do his job satisfactorily. A job specification is concerned with the job itself and not with the individual holding the job. It is intended to help illuminate the weaknesses of the job holder and help determine the skills and knowledge he needs to obtain to fulfil his job requirements. Alternatively, specifications can be based on an examination by behavioural scientists of people who are successful and efficient in their work. The United States Army once carried out a study to determine the attributes of an effective non-commissioned officer and the desirable model in the final analysis was judged to be an experienced, battle-hardened NCO. The analogy is not inexact.

KEY RESULTS AREAS

Only a proportion of any one man's activities leads to significant results; an often quoted figure is that 20 per cent of the activities influence 80 per cent of the results. It is important, therefore, to identify key results areas—that is those activities in which the individual's efforts will prove most effective. Priority should be placed on those activities in which results are most vital in achieving the main objectives of the company. From this exercise it is only a short step to selecting short term objectives.

Examples of key results areas would include such activities as:

1   Cost reduction
2   Development of subordinates
3   Communication
4   Physical layout
5   Information
6   Facilities
7   Organisation
8   Budgeting
9   Output

Key results areas within the Joseph Lucas Organisation are related to the results shown in "Scope" on the job description and are identified by alpha codes which are then used to link the objectives set with the key results areas (see Figure 2:3).

SETTING OBJECTIVES

Having established the main responsibilities of a job and its key results areas, the next step is to determine the individual's principal work objectives for the following year. Management by objectives is a very complicated process and in any detail beyond the scope of this book. Basically, the concept of management by objectives is intended to provide individual goals, but still leave considerable scope for initiative so that efforts are concentrated on achieving results rather than being determined by personal inclination. The system also gives the individual a greater sense of participation in determining his own training needs and self-development.

The number of objectives set for each individual should be no more than seven or eight; three or four could suffice. It is unlikely that any more would make any really significant contribution to company achievements. Objectives should in total represent a reasonable challenge to the individual, however. Some objectives may be of short duration while others can extend over more than one year.

Examples of objectives may be found on the performance appraisal form illustrated in Figure 2:4 which is, in fact, related to the job description shown in Figure 2:3. The second column is used to express the job holder's achievements and performance against the agreed objectives. Together the job holder and his immediate superior then determine the reasons for any lack of success and insert any measures they consider necessary to overcome the problems, including training, in the third column.

The reporting manager consults with the training manager to decide how any training needs are to be met and the proposed measures are written on the back page of the form (see Figure 2:5).

A register is kept to record when each manager's job description, key results areas and objectives are agreed, to ensure that the programme is carried out properly (see Figure 2:6).

Whenever possible, objectives should be quantitative in order that the evaluation of achievements be as factual as possible. Vague phrases, such as "to make regular visits to customers," are virtually useless; these do not require any analysis. It would be much better to state: "to visit all six major customers at least once during the year." In Figure 2:4, for example, objective 3 would be rather loosely worded if it were written as "the present reject rate for goods inwards to be reduced to 4 per cent," since the *improvement* in quality would not be quantified.

Objectives can be expressed by quantity, quality, cost or, easiest of all, time, although the use of time does leave a problem of how to measure the other aspects. If targets were being listed for production management, for example, they might include improvement in machine efficiency, quality standards, optimum staffing, costs, waste standards, etc.

Whatever the measurement used, under no circumstances should the standards set as targets be imposed on individuals. They should be agreed by the job holder himself in consultation with his superior. Whenever possible, work groups should be encouraged to set their objectives together. It may be helpful to number objectives, but it should not be necessary to place them in order of priority.

Objectives and specifications may need revision in the course of a year in the light of changing circumstances and a procedure should be established to ensure that this is done on a regular basis.

PERFORMANCE APPRAISAL

Performance appraisals are used to measure the extent to which a manager has succeeded in attaining the objectives set out in his job description, in other words, to appraise the individual's performance against the objectives agreed. It is then possible to identify the skills and knowledge which need to be developed to improve the individual's effectiveness, at least in terms of the existing job requirements.

Performance appraisals not only reveal the training needs of individuals to do his job better, but provide the opportunity to determine new demands being made on him and reveal the strengths and weaknesses of the training schemes and the obstacles or other constraining factors which affect his performance.

Whether or not salary and promotion should be linked with performance improvement and development remains highly controversial, however, and is a question which has been discussed in great detail by many writers. While it may be more convenient to relate them, it may be, to borrow one commentator's phrase, that one is trying to kill two or three birds with one stone and missing them all. On the other hand, performance appraisals may come to be regarded lightly if no relationship is seen by the individual between performance and salary.

Performance reviews clearly need to be regular if they are to monitor progress. In general, a manager is appraised by his immediate superior, although sometimes the views of others are taken into consideration. Obviously, anyone carrying out an appraisal must be close enough to be acquainted with the person's work. Joseph Lucas and Perkins Engines use the son–father–grandfather relationship. That is, a man is appraised by his immediate superior and then by *his* superior who, at the same time, assesses the reporting manager's performance in developing his subordinates.

Performance of management is more difficult if not impossible to measure, especially at the higher levels of the hierarchy where performance is less easy to define. Moreover, there may be opposition to appraisals, both from the managers whose performance is being appraised and the managers who are asked to make value judgements on another man's ability. Managers do not normally like to sit in judgement and, while it may be possible for them to make an evaluation, they find it difficult to put it in writing and be able to defend it. They are afraid of the impact adverse comments would have on a man's self-esteem and subsequent performance.

Unless the purpose of job appraisal schemes is clearly understood by all levels of management, they become indifferent to the programme and blame lack of time or pressure of "more important work" when they fail to cooperate. It may be helpful to involve a number of managers in the design of the appraisal form and in the development of the procedures and standards, so that they may understand the objectives of the scheme and their relationship to the total business operation. This helps to obviate any scepticism and difficulties when the forms are introduced.

The Joseph Lucas Organisation conducts a series of seminars for reporting managers to explain the techniques involved and the basic purpose of the appraisal form. They are given guidance on writing job descriptions and identifying key results areas, setting objectives, identifying training needs and proposing training/development measures.

At Joseph Lucas, where the emphasis is on improving performance in the existing job, the appraisal procedures consist of a sequence of events linked with the Group's fiscal year. Two copies of the performance evaluation form are distributed each June by the executive development officer for each manager and supervisor covered by the scheme. One copy is for use by the reporting manager through the year as a working document. The second copy is normally retained for completion and returned to Training by mid-September the following year.

At Joseph Lucas, objectives of departmental and functional managers are made to agree with those of the product general manager, each of whom has total responsibility for a product or group of similar products from inception to sale. This procedure of agreeing objectives of an individual with his immediate superior is repeated at each subsequent level of managers as necessary.

The objectives of the product general managers are based on relevant policy statements which they are expected to have. While objectives may comprise some which are directly related to the product, they may also include other areas of management concern not directly related to output, such as the development of subordinates. Corporate objectives are developed *after* the coordination of individual and functional objectives; in other words, company objectives are based on the results the product general managers and their managerial support are expected to achieve.

APPRAISAL FORMS

Whether or not formal documents need to be used in appraisals is still a highly controversial point. It seems likely that the industrial training boards will require them in the future for the purpose of general grant. There are advantages in having a standard form, even in small firms where the chief executive knows his managers personally. This is to ensure that review and a dialogue between managers and their subordinates are continuously taking place and that attention is given to the development of every individual. Moreover, they provide an opportunity for serious counselling, taking into consideration personal ambitions.

While appraisal procedures and appraisal forms may appear to vary widely from company to company, they all in fact have common features and differ only in the degree and sophistication of details sought. The format should be as simple and uncomplicated as possible. Basically, the purpose of an appraisal form is:

1   To help the senior manager to make an unbiased and accurate statement of his subordinate's recent performance
2   To determine the areas of strength and weakness which require attention by specific or general training
3   To identify areas where current performance could be improved, either immediately or after training

Only essential and relevant questions should be included; they should be carefully phrased and not beg the "right" answer. Some forms used also list the control criteria used to measure performance against each target and sometimes a column for suggestions or for appraisal comments by the senior manager.

An example of a management appraisal form has already been shown in Figure 2:4. Figure 2:8 is a further good example. Figure 2:9 shows an example of an appraisal summary based on the same performance and on the appraisal report shown in Figure 2:10.

STAFF APPRAISAL

The form used by Joseph Lucas (Figure 2:4) lists on the first page the objectives and the procedures to be followed in completing the form. Detailed information on completing the form is contained in *Notes for the Guidance of Supervisors*, a booklet manual distributed to supervisors. The other form, Figure 2:8 is used by Perkins Engines for selection of qualified personnel for promotion and for determining wage increases. Two forms are completed for each individual, one for the appropriate director and the other for the department or division concerned. Information up to "assessment" is completed by the staff member himself. Assessments can be made by several people who are distinguished by different coloured pencils or ink.

In many firms the man assessed signs the appraisal form to the effect that he has discussed and agreed the evaluation of his achievements, and that he has been informed of the overall evaluation of achievement. If a man is not informed of his evaluation, he may either consider it to be poor and express his frustration in grievances or, depending on his personality, believe that the grade must have been acceptable and has nothing to worry about. However, an American survey revealed that praise, in fact, had little effect in improving performance while adverse comments could have a negative effect. Those informed that they have poor performances are not encouraged to leave, as might be expected, but lost confidence and decide to remain where they are.

Where the job holder has an additional, functional, superior, he is involved whenever appropriate and must add his signature to the form.

ASSESSING POTENTIAL

There is not necessarily a close link between performance and potential, so that it may be advisable to introduce special procedures to recognise potential only after a performance appraisal scheme has become well established.

Nevertheless, an assessment of potential is necessary for promotion and succession planning and, wherever possible, to develop individual skills and knowledge and the best attitude for taking on greater responsibilities. It is not good enough to put all potential managers on a basic development course. This may be the reason why descriptions of existing jobs do not change very much. If training is to be of any value, there must be a clear understanding of the type of job a man is being developed for.

In appraising a man's performance, the reporting manager should at the same time make a judgment—necessarily in a broad and subjective way—on what the man may be capable of in the future, drawing on his past performance where relevant, but looking particularly at his strengths and weaknesses and his capacity for development. In this way it should suggest answers to such questions as:

1   Should he be transferred and, if so, where?
2   Is he ready now for promotion?
3   Is some form of training or guidance needed in order to fit him for transfer or promotion?
4   Are there any personal factors, such as bad health, unwillingness to move and so on to be considered in planning his career?
5   What are his own ambitions and interests and how far are the company's plans for him consistent with them?
6   Can his own job be restructured to give him more responsibility and allow him to grow?

It is unlikely that sophisticated or "objective" guides can be developed to determine either the suitability or capability of operators to be retrained. Very often there is simply no choice.

Corah Limited, whose knitwear manufacturing operations fluctuate with the vagaries of fashion trends, pays greater heed to the supervisor's knowledge of an individual's strength and weaknesses than to their personal records. Individuals are interviewed by personnel several months before they are scheduled to be retrained and, wherever possible, they are shown the different work available and are given a choice. The trainee's background and experience are studied, however, to help determine which instructional techniques ought to be used on retraining courses.

Within the Dowty Group all management appraisal forms marked "outstanding" are automatically brought to the attention of the personnel director who arranges to meet the reporting manager to ask the reasons why the man was rated in this way and to discuss his personal history record.

At Joseph Lucas, the emphasis throughout the appraisal procedures is on improving performance in the existing job. A separate form is completed on each individual to assist managers to recognise their subordinate's potential as objectively as possible. The information required in this document is supplementary to the performance evaluation. Ordinarily, reporting managers arrive at their final assessment in consultation with the executive development officer who must sign the form.

Until recently, Perkins Engines had a career panel which interviewed each apprentice once a year for three years after completion of his apprenticeship to determine potential and career development. Although the system proved useful the panel has become defunct mainly because of the difficulty in getting the various managers together. The company has taken precautions to ensure that ex-trainees do not suffer as a result, however, by putting up notices announcing vacancies and seeking people interested in becoming supervisors. Names may be submitted by individuals or recommended by their immediate supervisors. All applicants are interviewed by a supervisory selection panel and given a battery of tests.

IMPROVING ORGANISATIONAL APPROACH

These methods of identification of individual training need to be supplemented by a more comprehensive and continuous analysis, however. Indeed, it must be said that there are those, including some highly reputable training experts, who consider the methods described as an extremely naive and mechanistic approach to training and frankly doubt whether they can be wholly successful. These writers reject the idea that much time should be spent carrying out analyses of individual skills and knowledge as a "one off exercise." Moreover, rarely does a job description adequately reflect the total job requirement, they argue. A job description has no dimension, oversimplifies the complexity of the job, and ignores the social and psychological pressures and other factors affecting the job. And while most managers are able to describe their duties, responsibilities and their relative importance clearly, they miss the informal "social" or "human" requirements of their jobs which are considered equally important. In effect, it is like "taking out one important component, re-machining it and putting it back in a defective or inefficient machine."

What is needed is a deeper probe into the job environment, analysing the working methods, the obstacles to improvements in performance, the problems arising and the development plans which are likely to affect the jobs.

It may be necessary for training to act as a change agent and identify the fundamental changes which must be made in existing work situations and circumstances before training can prove effective. Improved skills and knowledge may be only one of several solutions, in fact, and perhaps not the best. It may, for example, be more beneficial to reconstruct jobs or working arrangements. It may be necessary to introduce more modern systems and procedures, new machinery or to improve the organisation and the lines of responsibility and communication.

This requires a continuous investigation of the work situation and problems with the identification of controllable factors on an interdepartmental basis. The problems may well arise through lack of coordination between two or more departments; improvements in one area may create difficulty in another. It may also be necessary to resolve conflicts which arise between departmental and company needs. It is then essential to determine the best means, possibly but not necessarily training, for achieving these. This leaves the field clear for defining the *real* training needs, including those created by changes and improvements made through other means.

All this requires a continuous study of departmental and interdepartmental activities, since after all rarely is an activity confined to one manager or within one department. It requires penetrating questions regarding efficiency and costs. It is necessary to identify causes of bottlenecks, for example, high setting and reclamation costs, work rejection or poor dispatch performances. It may be useful to study departmental reports regarding output, earnings, negligent accidents, labour costs, rectification costs, etc.

ASSESSMENT REPORT

It may be feasible to prepare a report covering the main conclusions of an assessment scheme, based on an analysis of the data collected and the problems identified which may be solved totally or partially through training. This report should cover the main conclusions of the assessment, indicating the size, nature and priority of the establishment's needs. Details of the information and evidence used to arrive at these conclusions should be included wherever necessary.

Training needs should then be listed in order of priorities and used to set training objectives. The following questions may help to determine the order of priority:

1   How serious is the problem?
2   What effect will it have on the establishment?
3   How much is it costing?
4   How long will it take to solve the problem? (This can be indicated as either short term or long term)
5   How will the costs of solution compare with the probable benefits

Nature of jobs	Staff required		Apparent deficit	Add to apparent deficit			Apparent vacancies to be filled	Deduct possible promotions from within	Total vacancies to be filled
	At present	5 years ahead		Retirements	Possible leavers	Promotions or transfers			
Production managers	2	3	1	1	—	1	3	1	2
Shift managers	4	6	2	—	—	1	3	—	3
Sales managers	2	2	—	1	—	—	1	1	—
Salesmen	6	10	4	2	2	1	9	—	9
[Others]									

FIGURE 2 : 1   EXAMPLE OF MANAGEMENT MANPOWER PLAN

This example shows a form for a management manpower plan which may prove satisfactory for a medium-size firm. In larger firms, it would be advantageous to subdivide jobs according to their specific background, technological, engineering or sales and so on, and to elaborate the table accordingly

Department_____

Manager/Supervisor_____

Date _3-1-67_ Revised on | 5-3-67 | 10-9-67 | 2-1-68 |

No & name	Service			Other depts	Jobs A	B	C	D	E	F		TWI JI / TWI JR	Remarks
	In ind	In firm	In dept										
J WHITE Charge hand	14	10	8		✗	✗	✗	✗	✗	✗			Retires 15-9-68
S BROWN	10	5	5		✗	✗	✓ T⅓	✓ T⅙	✓	✗			Replace WHITE Train by 1/9
R GREEN	3	3	3		✓P T⅓	✓	✓ T⅓	✗	✗				
T BLACK	2	1	1		✗	✓	T⅘/5	✓	✓				On Course 8-15/2/68
M BLUE	3	2	1		✓P T⅓		✓P T¼						Transfer if no improvement
F PINK	5	1	1		✓								Joined 1/1/68
													2 extra men needed for job C by 1/5/68

✓ Some exp   ✗ Fully able to do the job

FIGURE 2 : 2   TRAINING NEED RECORD

Part 1

Confidential

PERFORMANCE EVALUATION FORM

Name _____ *E.B. Ford* _____ Company _____ *BRZ* _____

Date of appointment
to present job _____ *1 February 1970* _____

Product group or function _____ *LMN* _____

Department _____ *Quality* _____

Part 2   Job description

Title   *Quality and Reliability Engineer*

Responsible to   *Product General Manager*

Directly supervising   *Three Quality Foremen*

Scope   *Ensures conformity to design specification by the economic appli-
                         cation of quality control and inspection techniques at all the neces-
                         sary stages of the manufacturing cycle, keeping scrap, rectification
                         and returns to a minimum.
                         The establishment and maintenance of appointed standards of relia-
                         bility (in conjunction with the Chief Engineer).*

Resources

Manning   *Staff 4, Works 142*

Finance   *Departmental Budget: £150 000*

Key results areas (A, B, C etc)

A *Stimulation of action to avoid excessive scrap and rectification*

B *Reduction of returns of original equipment and service failures*

C *Development of inspection methods for materials and bought out
  parts*

D *Operation of inspection procedures specified by official agencies*

E *Ensuring that appropriate major Mechanical and Electrical Test
  Equipment is obtained*

F *Development of subordinates*

FIGURE 2 : 3   JOB DESCRIPTION FORM, JOSEPH LUCAS

The job title is the same as that which appears on the organisation diagram. Under "resources" are entered the total number of people within the job holder's control, the limit of financial authority (if he is responsible for capital expenditure), and the departmental budget if he is responsible for one

Financial year   August _1970_ to July _1971_

Part 3   AGREED OBJECTIVES, RELATED ACHIEVEMENT AND TRAINING NEEDS ANALYSIS

Date of final agreement _10 August 1970_   Signature of _____   Signature of _____
of objectives   job holder   reporting manager

Key results area	Objectives	Achievement	Training needs analysis
See part 2	Specify and quantify objectives clearly and simply	Express achievement against agreed objectives	Specify any training needs identified in comparing achievement with objectives
A	1 To have arranged at least six Quality Sub-Committee meetings from which specific proposals to reduce scrap emerge	1 Objective met formally. Although proposals to reduce scrap were made, inadequate follow-up action was taken. Nevertheless the agreed level of the Factory scrap index was satisfactory	Further formal training as a practical engineer is not required
B	2 To reduce the number of original equipment returns by 10%		The failure to meet objective 5, and the partial success in 1 and 3 indicate insufficient ability in planning and organising work, and in controlling activities
C	3 The present reject rate for goods inwards to be reduced from 5% to 4%	2 This target was achieved at a figure of 12%. There were fewer customer complaints	Mr White must be helped in developing his self-confidence
D	4 No serious complaints on the operation of those inspection procedures specified by outside agencies	3 The required improvement was made. Yet the number of complaints made against bought out parts increased	
E	5 To have budgeted for the requirements for new test equipment in respect of new product TAF 4A, and ensured that all essential equipment had been obtained in time	4 Objective met – no serious complaints received 5 When the new product range TAF 4A was introduced in May 1971, three items of test equipment were not available	

Overall evaluation of achievement: Outstanding ☐   Very good ☐   Satisfactory ☒   Weak ☐   Unsatisfactory ☐

(The signature below indicates that the achievement and training needs analysis has been discussed and agreed with the job holder, and that he has been informed of the overall evaluation of achievement

Job holder _____   Date _16 August 1971_

FIGURE 2 : 4   PERFORMANCE EVALUATION FORM, JOSEPH LUCAS

Part 4   Development And Training Measures

In the light of the training needs analysis set out in Part 3, define specific training and/or development measures which may help the individual improve his performance in his present job

Wherever possible these measures should be defined in consultation with the training department

Proposed Measures

Mr White's training will be concerned particularly with: setting clear objectives, planning work, organising work, control of activities and contributions to team performance

His training should be in two parts:

1   On the job guidance and coaching aimed principally at improving planning and organising work, and control of activities

2   An external course on quality management with some emphasis on the organisation to ensure achievement of quality standards. Such a course is run by the Urwick Management Centre: duration one week

Part 5   Potential

Is this man promotable to a more senior position in a specialist or management role?   Yes* ☐   No ☐

If so, is he promotable within 3 years?   Yes ☐   No ☐

* The executive development officer will require the completion of an assessment of potential form for use by the executive development committee.

Signature of reporting manager

Signature of functional manager
(where a Functional Responsibility is
listed in Part 2 of this form)

Date_____

Date_____

FIGURE 2 : 5   TRAINING RECOMMENDATIONS, JOSEPH LUCAS

The training measures recommended to meet the needs identified on the form shown in Figure 2:7 are entered here. The lower part of the form concerns potential and is completed by the reporting manager

TRAINER'S REGISTER

Product group/department _____ Date _____

Senior manager concerned _____

Name	Appointment	Items agreed		
		Job description	Key results areas	Objectivoc

FIGURE 2 : 6   TRAINER'S REGISTER, JOSEPH LUCAS

Main responsibilities	Target performance	Job problems	Special action
List the main areas of responsibility (e.g. customer contact, production of detail drawings, etc). Between four and eight result areas, not a complete job description	Describe your objectives for each of the main responsibilities of the job. Give quantified targets, priorities, or planned improvements where possible	Identify recurrent problems which affect performance and limit your ability to achieve your objectives	Any special action required, arising from columns 2 and 3
1 *Production of manufacturing drawings and parts lists*	1 *To issue manufacturing drawings without errors and within target requirements*	1(a) *Shortage of draughtsmen* (b) *Constant alteration of design schemes whilst detail drawings are being produced* (c) *Lack of necessary information*	1(a) *Try to borrow draughtsmen from other drawing offices within the group* (b) *Avoid detailing schemes until they are complete and approved* (c) *Improve communications and, in particular, ensure drawing office instructions are clear and complete*
2 *Compilation and maintenance of design standards and procedures*	2 *To achieve up to date procedure' and standards manuals*	2(a) *Shortage of labour* (b) *Constant change of procedures to suit customer's requirements*	
3 *Production of technical manuals*	3 *To issue manuals as required, and keep up to date*	3(a) *Obtaining information from other departments* (b) *Shortage of a technical author*	
4 *Control of drawing modification procedure*	4 *To issue modifications which are accurate and easily understood*	4(a) *Lack of understanding by draughtsmen of the procedures* (b) *Lack of understanding by senior personnel and management, of the procedures*	4 *Educate the draughtsmen. Talks by assistant chief draughtsmen and section leaders*
5 *To provide a reference drawing and printing facility*	5 *To provide a rapid service and to avoid "waiting time"*	5 *Lack of a loan print facility*	5 *Loan print facility must be provided*
6 *Co-ordination within the design and drawing office*	6 *To ensure the optimum use of D.O. labour and services including forward planning and estimating*	6 *Forecasting of requirements and loads difficult, as design targets are never met*	
7 *Co-ordination with other departments, i.e. production, development, commercial*	7 *Control of manufacturing standards to the satisfaction of production and design departments*	7 *Control problems introduced by starting to manufacture in advance of establishing the customer's final requirements*	7 *To make drawing office staff more aware of the needs of the production departments. This would be achieved by informal coaching rather than formal training*
8 *Working relations within the department*	8 *To maintain good working relations, and negotiate with the trade union as necessary*	8 *Group policies not clearly enough defined – varying interpretations by individual companies and departments*	8 *Personnel department co-ordination required*

FIGURE 2 : 7   MANAGEMENT APPRAISAL FORM, DOWTY GROUP

This is, in fact, the inside two pages of a four-page management appraisal form. The first page is used for the job description and the back page to recommend training or experience needed, taking into consideration the objectives and priorities and including such activities as private reading. Columns 4 and 5 are completed jointly by the manager and the senior manager

Strictly confidential

Assessment of performance and potential

Name _____ Date of birth _____

Present position _____

Date appointed to present position _____ Date joined the company _____

Qualifications _____

Work history (this company and previously)

Dates	Job	Company	Salary

Assessment completed by   Date

Reviewed by   Date

---

1 Job objectives

List the objectives or most significant tasks for which he has been accountable during the period covered by this assessment. Refer to position description wherever possible

2 Results achieved

What results have been achieved against each objective or task? State the results achieved briefly giving examples and quantitative information where possible

3 Performance comments

This column enables variables beyond the employee's control affecting results to be identified, together with other relevant comments. Comment on the results achieved as necessary, *identify and underline* particular strengths, weaknesses in performance or inadequacies of skill and knowledge that require remedial action

Brief comments (two sentences)	Summary on strengths	Summary on weaknesses
Technical skills — *(Is he well qualified for the position? Is he learning?)*		
Management skills — *(How good is he at priority setting, risk taking, supervising and controlling work and people?)*		
Relationship skills — *(How does he "get on" with people?)*	Summary of development and training needs — what management action is required?	

FIGURE 2 : 8   COMBINED PERFORMANCE AND POTENTIAL ASSESSMENT FORM, PERKINS ENGINES

1   **Overall results in relation to job objectives**

Assess overall performance in relation to the results achieved in the employee's area of accountability. In making this assessment consider his performance in relation to how you expect him to perform considering his training and experience. On no account consider his performance in relation to that of other people

Note that a man rated as meeting expectations must meet the demands of his position in full. A positive degree of achievement, creativeness and reliability is to be expected

Exceeds performance expectations   ☐

Meets performance expectations   ☐

Somewhat below performance expectations   ☐

Substantially below performance expectations   ☐

2   **Performance changes since last assessment**

Greatly improved   ☐   Improved   ☐   Static   ☐   Declined   ☐

3   **Assessment of potential**

Indicate your assessment of the individual's potential for greater responsibility by marking the appropriate category below

Mark one box only

Better suited to present level of
responsibility rather than for   ☐
greater responsibility

Suitable for a job of greater
responsibility at his present level   ☐
in the organisation

Promotable one level higher than his   ☐
present level in the organisation

Promotable two levels higher than his   ☐
present level in the organisation

4   **Other positions to which promotable**

Positions anywhere in this company to which he might be promoted or for jobs to which he might be better suited

Disregard the availability of the job — consider only the man's potential

Position   *State how long you consider
it will take before he is
ready for this position*

FIGURE 2 : 8—*continued*

Job title	*Production Manager*	
Department	*Engraving*	

Name	*Mr B Sanders*
Date of appraisal	*17 March 1971*
Person carrying out the appraisal	
1 Name	*Mr H Goodwin*
2 Position	*General Manager*

Appraisal Report	Action agreed to help development of individual
Budget preparation has presented some difficulties	*Short external appreciation course followed by help from accounts*
Has increased recognition of need of small work teams	*Assign graduate trainee to assist him in study of layout of physical facilities* *Suggest book on job enrichment and employee motivation*
Some resentment to constant need for changes and short production runs	*Short course on marketing for non-marketing managers* *Arrange for regular attendance at marketing strategy committee meetings*
Unable to make quick decisions, as he himself admits	*Suitable external course* *Suggest Kepner-Tregoe*

FIGURE 2 : 9   EXAMPLE OF APPRAISAL REPORT

Name	*Mr B Sanders*
Adviser present at interview	*Mr A Trufant*
Date of appraisal	*17 March 1971*

Overall appraisal

Since his promotion to production manager some six months ago, Mr Sanders has shown himself to be well in command of the departmental activities and has earned the respect of his subordinates for his ability and fairness

Promotion potential

Never ☐   Perhaps ☐   Not yet ready ☒   Ready now ☐

To what staff level do you think he will rise?
At least one grade higher

Proposed action

1 Immediate   *Recommend suitable reading and implement the action agreed as early as possible*

2 Long term   *Arrange participation in policy making committee and prepare him for eventual attendance on management course*

Comments

As Mr Sanders is relatively new in his present position, he still lacks confidence and some weaknesses are apparent. Undoubtedly, he will be strengthened by the action recommended

Much has been done to improve working conditions and the working environment and the number of accidents has declined partly as a result of his efforts. This responsibility should probably be handed to his assistant so that Mr Sanders may concentrate on work arrangements

Signed   (signature of superior)

FIGURE 2 : 10   EXAMPLE OF APPRAISAL SUMMARY REPORT

3

Processing the Individual

An employer who wishes to qualify for a general grant from an industrial training board *must*, from the beginning of each grant year, maintain a training register of quantity and quality of training given and must produce up-to-date records for a training board's inspection as required. Training not supported in this way cannot be reported for grant claims.

REQUIREMENTS FOR TRAINING REGISTER

Generally the training boards demand the following information for the training register:

1   Name of person being trained
2   Age, if under twenty-one
3   Occupation for which he or she is being trained
4   Description of course being followed
5   Length and dates of course, giving number of days' training
6   Details of day and block release for further education where appropriate

The Knitting ITB further requires the trainee's national insurance number, the registered number of the approved instructor and starting date of employment.

Strip index cards intended for compiling a training register are available from Kalamazoo Limited. See Figure 3:1.

It is also useful to indicate whether training is given on or off the job. If training is on the job the record should indicate whether the items recorded relate to wholly supernumerary training or whether the period consists of on-the-job experience, for example, or whether training contributed to production. The board's assessors may wish to know this. The record can also include periods spent in off-the-job training, at management courses for example, or within the company, at discussions, talks and courses conducted by senior managers and specialists. Figure 3:1 is a sample register of trainees recommended by the Engineering ITB.

A syllabus of training is also required by every training board for every individual listed on the register. In the case of employees on a formal training course, a code may be used to refer to the appropriate training programmes which should be kept available for inspection by the boards' assessors.

The boards also require all those involved with giving training to be enumerated. These may be categorised as:

1   Training officers
2   Instructors
3   Supervisory staff
4   Others: clerical staff employed in the training department, for example

PERSONAL RECORDS

The industrial training boards have made no attempt thus far to impose any rules concerning the type of personal records to be kept, although several boards provide their members with a guide and sample record cards.

Figures 3:2 and 3:3 show standard record forms available from Kalamazoo. Standard forms can also be obtained from a number of trade and employers' associations.

Personal record cards are also used by a number of companies to record test results and personal achievements. Perkins Engines record training results on the front of its form and quarterly assessments on the reverse side. The form used by the Dowty Group, is also used to record training college progress on the reverse side.

There is no reason why trainee record cards should not be extended to become regular employment records, to be transferred to personnel once training is recorded. This obviates the need for personnel to maintain duplicate information. They would merely keep on file an empty envelope or a distinctive card with the trainee's name, date of birth, date of engagement and a reference to the effect that the personal file was held by training. All records and communications are forwarded to personnel at the end of training, except those for apprentices who continue on day release after completing their apprenticeships.

Personal history cards can include such particulars as age, health, mobility, education, qualifications, specialised technical skills, experience before joining the firm, appointments held within the firm, training received within or outside the firm, correspondence or evening courses successfully completed, hobbies and interests, professional membership, etc. Photographs on each record help to identify former trainees when discussing them years after completion of training. Perkins Engines photographs applicants in groups of eight or nine at the time they are being interviewed and each individual is then cut out of an enlargement. A copy is pasted on the application form to ensure that the same individual is being discussed by the selection committee.

Personal data recorded on the personal record cards are usually obtained from the trainee's application form and completed immediately as a trainee is engaged. If CSE or GCE results are unknown at this stage the trainee should be requested to inform the company when they are known so that they may be recorded. Ideally the data for both the application form and the personal record should be in the same sequence to facilitate transcription and to minimise errors. Further suggestions on the design of forms may be found in other books in this series.

One form can be used by both personnel and training to avoid duplication but this invariably proves impracticable even when the training function is situated near the personnel office. The form for each could be the same and be completed at the same time, but the training function normally need to know a lot more specific information which is not recorded by personnel and, conversely, personnel record a lot of information, such as the names of children and relatives working for the firm, for example, which is of no use to training. It is possible to design a form specifying the basic data required.

Personal history cards can be coded to facilitate retrieval. Different coloured cards may be used to indicate year of intake. The date of birth can be important when completion of training or day release is related to age, or for birthday wage increases. However, training is usually informed of the date for such increases by salary administration or, more likely, by the employee himself.

FILING METHOD

There are no standard methods for filing personal training records. They may be filed in strict alphabetical order but it is normally more useful to divide them in some way. Joseph Lucas Organisation uses different coloured cards for each year of intake and files them separately. Perkins Engines keeps its records for apprentices and operators separately from the others which are kept alphabetically. The National Coal Board files its records numerically with a separate alphabetical cross-index system which is updated manually for starters, leavers and any changes in works numbers.

It may also be practical to divide records according to the categories established by the training board, each one of the categories further subdivided according to the company's training schemes. The categories established by the Engineering ITB for example are:

1 Managers
2 Works superintendents, departmental managers
3 Scientists and technologists
4 (*a*) Administrative and professional staff
 (*b*) Clerical staff
 (*c*) Office machine operators
 (*d*) Secretaries and typists

5 Supervisors, including foremen

6 Craftsmen in occupations for which a worker has usually qualified after a recognised period of apprenticeship or equivalent training

7 (*a*) Operators with approved training which lasts at least one week but not more than four weeks

 (*b*) Operators with approved training which lasts longer than four weeks

8 Other employees, excluding canteen staff

The category into which individuals are placed can have a significant effect on the size of grant received by the company, without varying the amount of training carried out according to the different weight placed on each category. It is surprising how easily a manager can become a technologist when necessary.

Records should be physically situated where they may be easily accessible to instructors. When a trainee transfers from one location to another, the training officer at the "leaving" location should send his records to the "receiving" location or the training department. Upon completion of training, personal records are usually sent to personnel.

Correspondence and documents concerning the trainee should be kept together with the personal record card, in an adjoining folder or together with the card in a transparent folder.

COMPUTERISED PERSONAL RECORDS AT NCB

Training and education records for all industrial employees in the coal industry and statistics derived from these records are produced on computer from the National Coal Board's computer centre. The centre is linked to seven computer centres equipped with nine "third-generation" computers. The appropriate ones act as input and edit points and, where necessary, pass data to another centre, receiving back the final output for printing.

Throughout the country there are thirty-two mining training centres, twenty-five engineering training centres and six combined centres where formal practical and theoretical instruction are given. For each colliery there is a colliery training officer responsible for the training and welfare of all persons, but especially juveniles, employed at the colliery.

The various schemes of training are controlled and supervised at each level of the NCB's organisation, area and headquarters. There is also a full time liaison officer in each of the areas. His duties are:

1 To liaise between the designated and headquarters computer centres and area establishments concerned (that is, collieries, workshops, training centres, and so on) for the purpose of coordinating input and arranging for special output via the "file interrogation" programme

2 To instruct staff in the correct procedures for the creation of training records and their subsequent updating

3 To initiate and supervise the take-over of existing manual systems by EDP
4 To ensure that input is being originated at units according to the timetable and that output is being examined and filed in the approved manner by carrying out periodical audits of unit records
5 To suggest, in the light of experience, to the area head of industrial training branches modifications and developments to improve the system
6 To ensure that any modifications are implemented
7 To give guidance and arrange assistance as the occasion arises
8 To send output received from the computer centres back to units

COMPUTERISED PROCEDURES AT NCB

The input system was simplified and improved in April 1970 so that area headquarters could discontinue to maintain training records manually. The training record itself was redesigned to show in plain English instead of code numbers the training given and qualifications obtained and to enable it to be used as an input form by the unit training officers.

Under the revised system eleven input forms were replaced by three:

1 The training record to be used:
 (*a*) To update or amend existing training records; *or*
 (*b*) As a blank, to be completed in part for obtaining the training record printed by the computer of a re-entrant or transferee
2 A form for multi-entry output (Form C282)
3 A list, issued in August of each year, giving the current works numbers of all students enrolled into technical education courses during the previous session and designed to permit the input of their examination results

The training record, which is also used as an output document, is issued automatically by headquarters computer services for each new employee, excepting those for whom no current training is necessary—for instance, office cleaners. The record, which is in duplicate, is preprinted with information on the manpower file: name, date of birth, National Insurance number, works number and location (see Figure 3:4).

Form C282, which is in duplicate, is completed similar to the training record and is used for all input other than that put on the training record. Data for different courses or locations may all be entered on this single form. It may also be used by the unit for special training courses at the unit level, at manufacturers' works courses and for enrolment into apprenticeship schemes when these are controlled at area level. When the form is used to input information about a number of trainees from the same location, or about trainees from different locations attending the same course, only the spaces in the first and last lines of the appropriate columns need to be completed, with the word "repeat" inserted between vertical arrows (see Figure 3:5).

Each area manager is given a guide to procedure in the form of critical path analysis with instructions on how the forms should be completed.

Input of documents—that is, training records and form C282—relate to accounting periods and the top copy of documents must be sent by each colliery to the area liaison officer by the Wednesday following the end of a period. Carbon copies of the input forms are retained by the local staff. After scrutiny to ensure, as far as is possible, that the forms are correctly completed, the area liaison officer sends them on to the head of processing at one of the eight designated computer centres. They are punched from the information contained in them, verified and sent to the computer centre at Cannock for processing. There, input scrutineers examine the input to ensure, again as far as is possible, that it is correct. If it is not correct it is amended if this is practicable or, if not, it is returned unprocessed to the area liaison officer with a query sheet so that differences may be resolved before the information is printed.

From the input, the following output is produced by Headquarters Computer Services:

On the third Monday of each accounting period there is produced:

1 Updated training records, including changes in works numbers
2 A list of men on the manpower file but not on the training file, and of men on the training file but not on the manpower file
3 A training record with only the top section completed for each man on the manpower file but not on the training file

At the end of each fiscal quarter, Headquarters Computer Services produce the following outputs:

1 A summary of training given during the previous quarter, showing by course, unit and area, with national aggregations, the numbers starting and completing training, the numbers prematurely terminating training, the reasons for termination, and the numbers in training at the end of each quarter
2 A summary of training and retraining due, showing by unit, with area and national aggregation, and by type of training, the names and numbers due for special types of training or retraining for each of the next four quarters, with a special indicator for those overdue at the beginning of the quarter
3 A summary—prepared partly from the manpower file—of recruitment and wastage of apprentices, by area with national aggregations, with cumulative figures for each quarter
4 A quarterly long term forecast—also partly prepared from the manpower file—of craftsmen becoming available from apprenticeships and of craftsmen retiring from each colliery, with area and national aggregation

Area lists of students enrolled into technical education courses during the previous session are printed each August, showing the current works number of each student. This is designed to permit the input of their examination results. In January, a summary of technical education is printed out, showing by course and by unit, with area and national aggregations, the numbers enrolled in technical college courses for the previous session, their examination results and the numbers enrolled for the current session.

The training and education printouts, together with the input forms, are sent the same week in which they are produced to the area liaison officer who ensures that the output is checked against the input. The process follows the system shown in the illustration below:

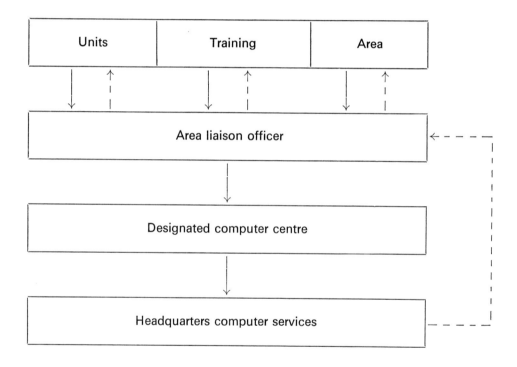

The area liaison officer examines the list of men who appear either on the manpower or training file and not on the other. It may be that the works numbers or other identification do not match, for example, or that the man has left the industry. When a man's name appears in the manpower file but not the training file list, it is generally because he is a new entrant, a re-entrant or a transferee.

When new output received has been checked and approved, the previous month's input and the previous training records which it replaces are destroyed.

NON-COMPANY TRAINEES

There should be no need to raise a standard form for trainees who are not employed by the company. In general these fall into four main categories:

1   Overseas trainees who have been sent to the company through an officially sponsored scheme by the British Government, the Confederation of British Industry or some other similar organisation
2   Sponsored trainees from subsidiary firms
3   Students from overseas countries who are sent to a company in exchange with the company's own trainees who have been posted abroad
4   University students who require a period of attachment to an industrial firm to obtain their degree
5   Employees of major customers who need to be trained as part of a sales agreement

Records of non-employees are normally kept separately. Perkins Engines make an exception for sponsored and vacation trainees from subsidiary firms who are treated as Perkins employees and included in the normal recording system.

Normally an introductory letter with the home and local address for each individual should be sufficient. At the completion of training a letter is usually sent to the trainee's sponsor stating that the trainee has completed the course or fulfilled any obligation. A copy of the letter, giving details of the training received, should be filed with any other correspondence in the personnel department. When a sponsor requires further details, however, the normal progressive forms should be put through for each trainee.

MANAGEMENT RECORDS

It is advisable to keep records of each individual manager who has undergone training or at least of the men who are thought likely to be worthy of development. The British Aircraft Corporation among others have basic supervisory and management courses and records are kept only on individuals who have successfully completed this course.

Many firms simply keep a list of courses and the course members in chronological order. This indicates who attended a particular course but makes no attempt to follow the training pattern of individuals.

Hawker Siddeley record the training undertaken by every individual on a separate card. See Figure 3:6. This form indicates every course attended, whether it is induction, familiarisation or specialist, the duration and the file index where a description of the course may be found. The form is found to be extremely valuable as a means of providing management with information which is really a by-product of its initial intent.

The information on these individual records is translated into a register each year by categories according to the classification used by the Engineering ITB. See Figure 3:7.

The name of each trainee is inserted on the register in chronological order according to the date in which he is enrolled. This is used to supply information to the Engineering ITB.

SELECTION OF TRAINEES

The training given can be only effective if those selected respond properly to training and prove capable of successfully completing the training in the required time, and are able to perform the work for which they are being trained. For this reason training must be concerned in recruitment and selection policies. The primary function of training, however, is simply training, and the details of recruitment and selection, including interviews, tests, and so on, are best left to specialists. Training should only be involved in so far as it is necessary to ensure that those engaged are properly qualified and fully understand the training and opportunities which are being offered by the company.

The objective of recruitment and selection methods should not necessarily be to obtain applicants with the highest qualifications, but those with the right characteristics and aptitudes. Procedures intended to seek only applicants of highest calibre may end up with an embarrassing imbalance of trained personnel and a high wastage among the best qualified.

Trainees with inordinately high pass rates begin to associate their technical college achievements with their career progress. Craftsmen who may have once been interested in seeking high salaries in tool rooms, aspire to greater things and want to become technicians, and rightly so. But the company is then embarrassed with too many technicians and too few craftsmen despite its well conceived plans. Not long ago, Dowty discovered that out of thirty apprentices, only three stayed on the shop floor. Consequently the Group lowered the intake level of its draftsmen in order to retain more of them as craftsmen.

In certain areas it may be necessary for training to establish prerequisites of various training schemes and courses. This requires drawing up a list of skills, knowledge and other basic attributes—intelligence, empathy, judgement, dexterity, visual acuity, strength, and so on—required for each job. The specifications not only aid selection procedures but help to reduce the number of applicants to those most qualified, thus reducing the work involved in interviewing and selecting unsuitable candidates.

These job specifications, which can be based on those used on job descriptions, can be used in recruitment advertisements and in recruitment literature, supplemented by details of the training programme, opportunities, prerequisites. These last would take in experience or qualifications needed before taking the course, specific practical training required before and after being placed, the type and extent of experience to be gained on the job and whether or not this implied specific training.

It is important, however, that the opportunities and chances of promotion after training are not exaggerated as frustration and high labour turnover may result when such expectations are not fulfilled. Recruitment literature should also, of course, give details of the company, salaries, benefits, general conditions of employment, etc.

A patterned interview form can serve as a useful checklist of job requirements when interviewing applicants. Judgements and predictions should then be made at the time of appointment and checked at a later date to see if they were correct.

RECRUITMENT PROGRESS CONTROL

The British Aircraft Corporation keep a wall chart to record the progress of all applications. The left-hand vertical column contains the name of each applicant. In adjoining columns each box is checked as appropriate:

1 Application received
2 Application rejected
3 Application withdrawn
4 Called for interview
5 School report
6 Rejected
8 Satisfactory
9 Provisional offer
10 Provisional acceptance
11 Firm offer
12 Not followed up

APPLICATION FORMS

Application forms for training schemes should differ from ordinary application forms and be designed specifically for the use of the training function. Whenever possible data requested on the application forms should be in the same sequence and in the same format as they are to be transcribed onto the personal form, again to facilitate transcription and keep errors to a minimum.

Conditions of employment, method of selection and space for interviewers' comments should if at all possible be included on the application form. An example of a well designed application form intended specifically for prospective apprentices is shown in Figure 3:8.

REFERENCE FORMS

It is doubtful if reference letters are very helpful in selection since most people dislike making derogatory remarks in any statement. References from headmasters concerning prospective apprentices are helpful, however.

Several firms send a standard reference form to the headmaster when a boy is short-listed. Figure 3:9 is an example of a standard form which headmasters are asked to complete. Standard reference forms are usually preferred by headmasters since they indicate precisely the information sought. Employers on the other hand have found less tendency on the part of headmasters to exaggerate achievements or embellish their remarks on standard forms and they can therefore be considered more accurate.

Time and energy can be saved by the use of standard form letters. The letter inviting an application for an interview should include instructions on where to report (including the gate number if there are more than one) and directions on how to reach the firm by public transport. Some firms include a prepaid postcard for the applicant to return, indicating whether he will attend the interview as arranged. If reimbursement of expenses is to be made this should be stated.

Letters of acceptance should give the date in which the applicant is due to report, instructions on where to report and any documents, such as a birth certificate, which he should bring with him. A brief history of the company, with a description of its products, working conditions and benefits should be enclosed.

Young trainees should also be provided with a statement of rules and regulations to be followed. Perkins Engines also encloses with its rules and regulations a declaration which must be signed by the apprentice and his parents stating that the boy has read the rules and regulations and intends to abide by them. The apprentices are formally advised upon engagement that the company reserves the right to terminate an apprenticeship for what it regards as a serious breach of these rules, but in fact disciplinary action is rarely taken and never without a careful examination of the case.

STARTING NOTICE

All forms to be completed by a trainee should be taken care of on his first day of employment. A standard form can be used to notify wages that an individual has started employment. These can be completed before trainees arrive. Each trainee should be given a copy of rules and regulations and conditions of employment, if they have not been issued previously. Brush Electrical provides each employee with a short statement indicating where specific information concerning employment and amendments are to be found.

INDENTURES

Indentures have been in use for some 900 years and, while efforts are now being made to introduce reforms in the traditional concept of apprenticeship, which is no longer adequate, it will not be easy to change so old a custom.

An indenture is an agreement between employer and apprentice to give and receive instruction. For an agreement to be interpreted legally as an indenture, however, it is necessary to show that the *primary* object of the contract is to give and receive instruction. The fact that an employer contracts to give instruction does not necessarily make the contract an indenture. The instruction must be the central feature of the agreement.

It is also a general principle of English law that any agreement with a minor, including indentures, must as a whole appear to be favourable to the apprentice. Intolerable conditions can no longer be imposed by employers as were imposed on poor young John Griffyn who, in 1421, in order to learn the art of weaving, had to sign an agreement "not to frequent taverns or bawdy houses, or play dice or chess, or commit adultery or fornication with his master's wife, daughter or servants."

Although it is customary for parents or a guardian to sign an agreement this is not strictly necessary. A minor cannot be sued in his own name, so any legal action would in any event have to be against the parent. Whether the contract is binding or not is a "question of fact" in law and must be determined in each individual case. In general an employer has no power to end the apprenticeship arbitrarily, and the trade unions normally take the line that the employer had ample time during selection process and during probation to establish the suitability of a boy. If a boy proves unsuitable, it is best to interview the parents and explain the situation and attempt to terminate the apprenticeship by mutual agreement.

An indenture should be regarded as the legal document which it is and be filed either in the apprentice's personal file or together in alphabetical order according to surname.

Standard indenture forms can be obtained from several of the employers associations, but these tend to be highly legalistic. Figure 3:10 shows a much simpler form used by the British Aircraft Corporation.

MEDICAL RECORDS

It is obviously important for the training function to know of any disabilities or physical weaknesses which make it impossible for an employee to complete his course or perform the work for which he is being trained.

Physical examinations are a costly procedure, however, and are looked upon with suspicion by some who fear their misuse. But it is important that medical problems which would make training unsuitable be revealed so that individuals may be properly assessed for other and more suitable work.

Details of health are usually solicited on application forms. In addition the British Aircraft Corporation gives to each applicant a questionnaire on health matters which must be completed. If a statement is proved to be a deliberate attempt to mislead the company the employee is subject to instant dismissal.

The extent to which physical examinations are given depends very largely on the health service provided by the company and the medical requirements for the work to be performed by the trainee. The physical requirements for each job should be included in any job analysis or job specification. These may require only a cursory examination of eyesight, the pulmonary system or tests for signs of tuberculosis tendencies. Where training is short and few problems arise it should not be necessary to introduce tests for anyone except those who may give cause for doubt.

All employees under the age of eighteen are required by law to receive a medical examination at least once a year.

Prospective apprentices at Perkins Engines are examined twice, once at the time of their interview and again when they begin work. He is examined initially to determine any limitations, colour blindness for example, which could affect his training programme. A boy with colour blindness would not be offered an apprenticeship in electricity, for example. Assuming he meets the necessary qualifications, an applicant is accepted for some other occupation and his instructors and supervisors are made aware of any problems which may cause difficulties.

A medical history card is usually kept by the health officer for every employee who has been examined. This form should record the date and type of examination given and the results. Sufficient space should be given to allow other information to be added as necessary. Any information intended to be confidential should be coded on any memoranda which leave the health office. If required, confidential information on an individual can be placed on a separate form so that only routine information is contained on the card completed by a typist.

ABSENCE REPORTS

Good attendance is particularly important for trainees undergoing a programme of training and absences should be noted to identify the specific training missed by an individual. Where separate in and out clock racks are used by trainees, absences can be quickly noted. Otherwise, a list of absentees and dates may be obtained from instructors on a daily or a weekly basis. Arrangements should also be made with the local technical college to provide the company with a record of attendance.

Attendance records for each individual may be noted on the trainee's personal record card or on a separate form altogether. The standard forms illustrated in Figure 3:11 is available from the HMSO. The form shown in Figure 3:12 is used by apprentices at Perkins Engines for any time taken off, including holidays. In the case of sickness the form must be accompanied by a health certificate.

At Ideal Homes, a bonus of £2.50 a month is offered apprentices for good attendance, timekeeping and conduct. These bonuses are awarded each month and the money is kept in the Accounts Department where it may be withdrawn by the apprentices to purchase books, tools or other materials related to work.

PLACEMENT PROCEDURES

At termination of training, it is often the responsibility of training to place trainees and sometimes negotiate wages. There should be no problems if the company and the industry have been discussed frankly at the interview and during induction training. Whenever possible, arrangements should be made during the course of training to show trainees around the works so that they may see experienced employees at work and to meet ex-trainees or other trainees on the job.

The Central Training Council recommends that the first managerial post should be one where the trainee is accountable for the results achieved and where there is some scope and opportunity for development of the work. The duration of "training" before this first placing may be based on a target period—for example, two years—but there should be reasonable flexibility so that the timing of the move matches the trainee's progress as well as the availability of suitable vacancies. Essentially the aim should be to give the trainee a job with responsibility as soon as he is ready for it. Even where the period of training is linked to a specific programme, such as industrial or commercial training associated with a course at a business school or one leading to a professional qualification, it should be possible to adjust the programme where necessary.

If possible, he should be assigned first to an area where he was not known as a trainee. It is important that such assignments be assessed for results.

In some firms, a standard form is used by departmental managers to notify training of any existing vacancies. There may occasionally be difficulty in finding suitable posts for employees completing training, however, and in these circumstances they should be given a temporary assignment for a set period or until a suitable vacancy arises. There should be no need to set up a special system for this problem, however. A note in a diary should suffice and in any event the trainee can normally be relied upon to keep reminding training of his "plight." Ordinarily, there should be no difficulty in placing trainees once their worth have been proven. In fact, some individual trainees are often requested by several managers.

In some companies apprentices are interviewed long before completing their training to help them select their own specialisation and where they wish to work. In the Joseph Lucas Organisation each apprentice is interviewed at the end of his first year off-the-job training and again at the end of each year. The apprentice's achievements are compared with his selection test results to establish the boy's strengths and weaknesses and his own preferences. Each time he is informed of the company's plans for him and his approval is obtained.

Apprentices at the Dowty Group are interviewed about nine months before completing apprenticeship and again after training.

PLACEMENT RECORDS

Personnel and salary administration are usually advised that a trainee has been placed through a standard form, a copy of which is retained in the trainee's personal file. In some firms authorisation must be obtained previously through a standard application form.

If properly designed, the same form can be used for initial placement, transfers, grade or salary changes. Figure 3:13 shows such a form used at Perkins Engines.

One form only is used at British Aircraft Corporation for any change whatsoever in the employee's status (see Figure 3:14).

When an employee leaves before completing training, a standard termination form can be used to notify personnel and salary administration.

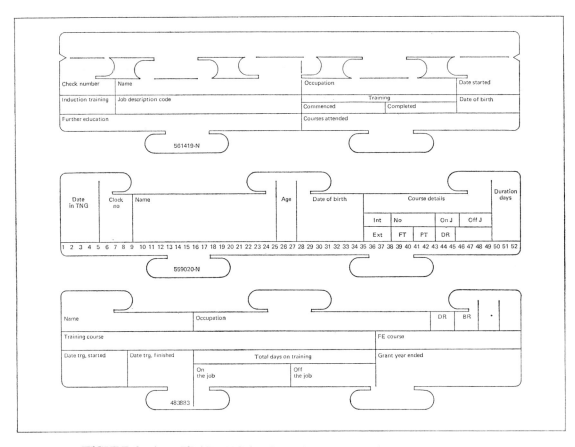

FIGURE 3 : 1   TRAINING REGISTER ENTRY CARDS, KALAMAZOO

Personal training form with the following fields and legend:

Code on visedge

Code	Meaning
M/F	Male or female
C	Carpets
S	SR
PP	Permanent press
K	Knitting
D	Dyeing
F	Finishing
CR	Crimp
MU	Making up
CT	Carpet task group
KT	Knitting task group
IE	Industrial evaluation
TM	Technical managers

Address / Tel number

Induction courses: Date — Course — Result — Comments

External updating courses: Date — Course — Comments

Address / Tel number

Practical induction training: Date — Place — Report from — Comments

Internal updating courses: Date — Course

Column headings along the edge (visedge):
Date of birth D|M|Y — M/F — C — S — PP — K — D — F — CR — MU — Date started D|M|Y — Area covered — Name — GT KT IE TM

1 2 3 4 5 6 7 8 9 10 11 12 13 14 15 16 17 18 19 20 21 22 23 24 25 26 27 28 29 30 31 32 33 34 35 36 37 38 39 40 41 42 43 44 45 46 47 48 49 50 51 52 53

FIGURE 3 : 2   PERSONAL TRAINING FORM, KALAMAZOO

47

Positions held

Education and training in other companies

From	to
From	to
From	to
From	to

In company off-the-job training

Course title or subject	Type of release	No of days	Dates From	Dates To	Instructor	Comments

External training

Course title or subject	Organising body and location	Academic year or level	Type of release	No of days	Dates From	Dates To	Result/comments

Sex M/F	Name	Initials	Date of birth	Department	Works no	Date joined company

FIGURE 3:3   PERSONAL TRAINING FORM, KALAMAZOO

48

TRAINING RECORD

FIGURE 3 : 4   PERSONAL TRAINING RECORD FOR COMPUTER, N C B

The "type of code" (columns 15 to 17) is used for recording an apprenticeship and various courses, statutory qualifications and appointments, including manufacturers' works courses. More than one sheet may be used for a trainee if necessary

INDUSTRIAL RELATIONS DEPARTMENT - TRAINING BRANCH

PERSONNEL RECORD — TRAINING : INPUT

Page number   of
Date submitted

Card class

1	2	3
7	0	1

Punch in all cards

Level of mgmt — 4 5
Location — 6 7 8
Act- ivity — 9
Works number — 10 11 12 13 14
Name and initials (block capitals)
Type of code — 15 16
Date commenced — Day 17 18, Month 19 20, Year 21 22 23
Indentures number — 24 25 26 27 28 29
Finished Date — Day 30 31, Month 32 33, Year 34 35
Code no — 36 37
Certificate number — 38 39 40 41 42 43 80

1 2 3 4 5 6 7 8 9 10 11 12 13 14 15 16 17 18 19 20 21 22 23

Number of line entries

Completed by _____ on _____

Punched by _____

Verified by _____

To be sent to the nominated computer centre not later than the 20th of the month

FIGURE 3 : 5   COMPUTER INPUT FORM, N C B

This form is used for all input other than that recorded on the training record

COMPANY TRAINING RECORD

Name ————————————————

Born ————————————————

Occupation ————————————————

EITB Category

1	2	3	4a	4b	5	6	7	8

Induction						
familiarisation						
specialist						

	1 Sept	31 Aug ————
Period	1 Sept	31 Aug ————
	1 Sept	31 Aug ————

File index	Course title	Location	Dates		Days on	Days off	Day or block	Remarks	Reg index
			Start	Finish					

FIGURE 3 : 6   COURSE ATTENDANCE RECORD, HAWKER SIDDELEY

1	2	3	4	5	6	7	8

Company training register   Grant year 1 Sept 19   to 31 Aug 19

Name of trainee	Date of birth	EITB classification	Training Induction Familiarisation Specialist	Location of course or training	Dates of course or training	Total number weeks or days	Day or block release
			A B C				

| Dept | M/S staff | Clock no | | 1 | 2 | 3 | 4a | 4b | 5 | 6 | 7 | 8 | Course title | A | B | C | | Start | Finish | Off | Job | On | |

FIGURE 3 : 7   COURSE ATTENDANCE RECORD, HAWKER SIDDELEY

52

This form must be completed by the applicant in his own handwriting	Office Use Only
Perkins Engines Company, Peterborough **APPRENTICE SCHEME APPLICATION FORM**	Category _____ Acknowledged _____ Headmaster's report requested _____

Surname _____

Christian names _____

Date of birth _____

Address _____
_____
_____

Parent or guardian

Name_____

Address_____
_____

Occupation_____

Relatives in company's employ

Name	Relationship	Dept

Have you made a previous application? If so give date

Schools attended	Dates	Sports, hobbies and other interests

Examinations passed	Date	Examinations to be taken	Date	Examining body

Details of subsequent employment or education
_____
_____

State of health_____

Any other information_____

Type of apprenticeship desired	Signature of applicant _____
	I have read the conditions overleaf and this application is made with my approval
	Signature of parent _____ Date _____ or guardian

FIGURE 3:8   APPRENTICESHIP APPLICATION FORM, PERKINS ENGINES

The Headmaster _____ _____ _____ _____		Date_____
Name _____ _____		Age _____

The above student has applied to us for a _____
Apprenticeship and we shall ask him to attend for an interview in the near future. To support his application we should be obliged if you would complete the following details which are relevant to his suitability for admission to our Apprenticeship Scheme. This report will be treated as a confidential document and will be destroyed if the application is unsuccessful

ACADEMIC ABILITY	
His present form	
If not in 6th form, average position in form during last two years	
If more than one stream state grade or title (e.g."A" or "5th Science" etc)	
His three best subjects in order of merit	1
	2
	3
PRACTICAL ABILITY	
Has he shown any skill in handwork, such as woodwork, metalwork, art or laboratory work? (Exceptional, good, average, poor)	
Interest in handwork (Exceptional, good, average, poor)	

FIGURE 3 : 9   HEADMASTER REFERENCE FORM, PERKINS ENGINES

PERSONALITY

Has he accepted responsibility in school life
e.g., prefect, captain, NCO, etc?

Does his work show any degree of inventive-
ness or originality?

Is he able to work satisfactorily without
supervision?

Has he fitted in well with school life or is he
difficult or selfish with others?

DETAILS OF EXAMINATIONS

GCE "O" level				GCE "A" level		
Subjects taken/ to be taken	Pass/fail or estimated pass/fail	If passed good/fair		Subjects taken/ to be taken	Pass/fail or estimated pass/fail	
1				1		
2				2		
3				3		
4				4		
5						
6						
7						
8						

Any other examinations taken/to be taken _____

GENERAL REMARKS

Signed _____

Date _____

FIGURE 3 : 9—*continued*

APPRENTICESHIP AGREEMENT

THIS APPRENTICESHIP AGREEMENT made the   day of   **19**   between
BRITISH AIRCRAFT CORPORATION LIMITED of 100 Pall Mall London SW1

(hereinafter called "the Corporation") of the first part

and

(hereinafter called "the Apprentice") of the second part

and

(hereinafter called "the Guardian") of the third part

WITNESSETH as follows:

1   THE Apprentice shall:

(a) *Enter into the employment of the Corporation at the   Works of the   Division with effect from   19   continuing until   19 (unless sooner terminated as hereinafter provided);*

(b) *Fully observe and comply with the Conditions of Employment for Apprentices in force at whichever Works of the Corporation he is employed from time to time (which said Conditions are deemed to be incorporated herein).*

2   THE Guardian hereby undertakes that the Apprentice shall duly perform and observe the obligations and undertakings on the part of the Apprentice to be performed and observed hereunder.

3   IN consideration of the undertakings hereinbefore contained the Corporation shall:

(a) *Take the Apprentice into its employment for the period mentioned in Clause 1 (a) hereof;*

(b) *Make available such facilities for the education and training of the Apprentice as the Corporation deems necessary with a view to the Apprentice acquiring under the Corporation's supervision a knowledge of*

(c) *Comply with the Conditions of Employment for Apprentices referred to above;*

(d) *Upon the completion of the Apprentice's training to the satisfaction of the Corporation issue to the Apprentice a Certificate to that effect.*

4   WHERE an Apprentice is to be transferred from one Works to another the prior agreement of the parties hereto will be obtained.

5   THIS Agreement may be terminated by the Corporation at any time free of all liability if for any reason:

(a) *The Apprentice fails to complete a six-month probationary period to the satisfaction of the Corporation;*

(b) *The Apprentice fails to perform and observe any of the obligations and undertakings to be performed and observed by the Apprentice hereunder;*

(c) *The Corporation is unable to perform its part of this Agreement for a cause which is reasonably beyond its control;*

(d) *The aforesaid Conditions of Employment for Apprentices so allow.*

IN WITNESS whereof this Agreement has been entered into the day and year first above written.

SIGNED by

of the   **Division**

for and on behalf of

BRITISH AIRCRAFT CORPORATION LIMITED

SIGNED by THE APPRENTICE ....

SIGNED by THE GUARDIAN ....

FIGURE 3 : 10   APPRENTICESHIP AGREEMENT, B A C

PUBLISHED BY H M STATIONERY OFFICE

Name	Dept	Check No

Year 19__/19__ | **ABSENCE RECORD**

HOURS ABSENT SHOWN— { Sickness (or accident) __ S Black Leave other than recognised holidays __ **L** Black

Reasonable excuse __ __ **E** Black Without reasonable excuse__Red (late arrival-Red encirced-($\frac{1}{4}$))

Month	1	2	3	4	5	6	7	8	9	10	11	12	13	14	15	16	17	18	19	20	21	22	23	24	25	26	27	28	29	30	31

Dates warned for bad timekeeping or absenteeism

MONTHLY SUMMARY

Month	HOURS OF ABSENCE					Total absence (including late arrival)	Total planned hours (including overtime)	% lost of planned hours (including overtime)	Number of occasions of late arrival under col (4)	Note of action taken
	Sickness or accident		Leave other than recognised holidays	With reasonable excuse	Without reasonable excuse						
	Cer-tified	Uncer-tified			Late arrival	Other					
	(1)		(2)	(3)	(4)		(5)	(6)	(7)	(8)	(9)
Total											

FIGURE 3 : 11   ABSENCE FORM, H M S O

Hourly Paid Apprentice Absence Form

To: Personnel
Time office

Clock number	Name	Department

Period of absence		Reason for absence
From — Time — Date		
To		
Number of working days		

Company business — paid		Private reason — excused paid	
Holiday entitlement — paid		Private reason — unpaid	
Sickness — paid		Signed by works supervisor _____	

Date _____ Approved _____

Apprentice training supervisor

This form must be completed to explain reason for any absence from work or technical college. To ensure payment for absence due to sickness, medical certificates for the period must be obtained

FIGURE 3 : 12   APPRENTICE ABSENCE FORM, PERKINS ENGINES

Please complete in triplicate
Copies 1 and 2 to Staff Personnel Manager
Copy 3 to be retained

PRIVATE & CONFIDENTIAL

Serial No

Staff Conditions - Change Note

Categories *A*, *B* or *C*

								Mr	Mrs	Miss
Name						Initials		☐	☐	☐

	Date of birth			Date com staff service			Date com present job		
Clock No	Day	Month	Year	Day	Month	Year	Day	Month	Year

	Present dept job	Proposed dept job			Present	Proposed
Dept Name			Location		Weybridge ☐	Hurn ☐
Dept. no					Hurn ☐	Weybridge ☐
Job title			Hours per week		37 ☐	40 ☐
Job code					40 ☐	37 ☐

	Present salary			Proposed salary			Increase type code	
	Amount	Staff cat	Scale	Amount	Staff cat	Scale	Tick where appropriate	
Weekly staff	£			£			1	General
Monthly staff	£			£			2	Scale minimum
							3	Scale adjust
Last salary increase	Day	Month	Year	Amount		Type	4	Merit
							5	Promotional
For salaries admin use only	Proposed effective date						6	Rate for age
							7	Off rate for age

Reason for proposal	Action	Routing	Name	Date
	Originator	Dept head		
	Approved	Director/nominee		
	Checked	Salaries administration		
	Approval for payment			
	Actioned for payment	For chief accountant		

PRIVATE & CONFIDENTIAL

STAFF CONDITIONS - CHANGE NOTE

Serial No.

From: **Staff personnel manager**

The changes proposed have been approved and will become effective on [ ]

The increase in salary will be included in the payment to be made on [ ]

The staff member concerned should now be informed

To_____

Dept_____

Signed_____

FIGURE 3 : 13   PLACEMENT FORM, PERKINS ENGINES

59

NOTIFICATION OF STAFF TRANSFERS, GRADE AND SALARY CHANGES

Name _____ Clock number _____ New clock number _____

| **Present conditions** | **New conditions** |
| | (Make entries only where changes are proposed) |

Division _____   _____

Department _____   _____

Section _____   _____

Location _____   _____

Budget centre _____   _____

Job title _____   _____

Job code _____   _____

Salary grade _____   _____

Salary range: Minimum   Maximum   Minimum   Maximum

Actual salary _____   Proposed salary _____

Amount of last performance increase _____   Amount of proposed increase _____

Date of last performance increase _____   Proposed effective date _____

Date appointed to job   _____   Is overtime payable

Date appointed to company   _____   (Monthly staff only)   Yes/No

Manpower classification   Manpower classification

(For completion by P & IR)   _____   (For completion by P & IR) _____

Reason for change or transfer _____

Name and clock number of employee replaced _____

REVIEWS AND AUTHORISATIONS

Originator	General Manager of Operating Unit
Signature _____ Date _____	
Title	Signature _____ Date _____
Other Authorisation (If Required)	Functional Staff Director
Signature _____ Date _____	
Title	Signature _____ Date _____
Other Authorisation (If Required)	Staff Director, P & IR
Signature _____ Date _____	
Title	Signature _____ Date _____
P & IR Salary Administration Review	Group Managing Director
Signature _____ Date _____	Signature _____ Date _____

FIGURE 3 : 14   CHANGE OF STATUS FORM, B A C

4

Implementation of Training Programmes

Having identified the training needs of the company and each individual, it is necessary to formulate a strategy for achieving specific objectives with emphasis on the training which has to be given priority to achieve company objectives. This requires some sort of outline or plan.

TRAINING PLAN

A training plan should have three basic aspects:

1   *The targets for the year based* on the priority of training needs and outlining the training to be provided. Targets for future years may also be included if desired

2   *Definite times by which training needs to be completed* to meet personal and company objectives, and the date each phase should begin to meet this deadline and avoid disruption in production

At Perkins Engines, the recruitment, selection and placement of trainees is included in the critical path network for every expansion scheme or critical project. Each stage is keyed on a day-to-day basis to a training programme which gives type of training needed, basic or advanced, off or on the job, and the end result required from the training.

3   *Responsibility for each aspect of training,* including the line manager involved, as well as those responsible for actually carrying out the training: training officers, instructors, supervisors, consultants, technical colleges. If an external course is to be used, this should be indicated

It is imperative that training arrangements do not become mechanistic, however. Training plans are intended to assist in administering and arranging training programmes, not govern individuals. Training must be given when the individual needs it or wants it, not at the convenience of the training function. This cannot be overemphasised.

TRAINING PROGRAMMES

The type of training, the syllabus and the training techniques to be used all depend very much on the type of trainees, the kind of organisation, the level of skills and knowledge required and the resources of the company. Generally, the decision is made by training in consultation with the man's immediate superior and sometimes with the man himself.

The written programme or syllabus giving details of training is, of course, required by the training boards for every employee included on the training register as supporting evidence of a general grant claim.

Training programmes take various forms but in general they should show clearly how the training needs of each job or each individual are being mct and the reason for each facet of training and its objective. In the case of existing managers, the programme of training should be specific to the needs of the individuals concerned. A training programme should contain, basically:

1   Course title
2   For whom it is intended
3   Objective or purpose of the training
4   Description of training
5   Duration and time schedule for each aspect
6   How the training will be applied
7   Follow-up arrangements: how the effectiveness of the training will be measured

The description of the training should include such details as projects, works visits, internal and external courses, training techniques used, and when training is given on or off the job.

At Brush Electrical, each graduate trainee is given a folder containing his training programme and several forms for recording individual progress.

Present experience indicates that training programmes should be retained for at least two years after completion.

The pattern of training is naturally subject to changes as qualifications or training board recommendations are altered. The training programmes should be kept up to date and amendments made immediate as alterations are introduced.

The pattern of training followed is very largely determined by company circumstances and resources. The decision on whether the company should conduct its own formal courses or use external courses, for example, is determined by many factors. To establish internal courses, it is necessary to consider availability of staff, facilities, the course content, and the cost. In considering external courses, it is necessary to take into account such factors as initial cost, course aims and qualifications, content, method, planning and preparation needed, staff, facilities, location, support provided by course organiser, provisions for follow-up, frequency course is given, and the ultimate cost. The importance of each will vary from firm to firm and each firm will have its own views on the relative importance of the criteria used. This of course presupposes that the firm is able to select the criteria and rank them in order of importance.

EXTERNAL COURSES

Courses sponsored and conducted by outside organisations vary considerably from one-day appreciation courses to residential courses lasting several weeks. There are at present some 500 organisations in this country offering more than 7000 different courses, many of which are repeated regularly. These cover such general subjects as finance, marketing and the like or more specialised techniques, such as work study, computer application or operational research. Some are intended for specialists and others on the same subject for the non-specialist.

Attendance at external courses should be reported to training so that they may be recorded for grant purposes. At Perkins Engines, all payment requests for external courses must be countersigned by the training department to ensure that they are informed of courses attended and to verify that the course is in fact taking place. Figures 4:1 and 4:2 show two different forms designed by Kalamazoo especially to record external courses, seminars and so on attended by company employees. A syllabus or programme for each should be attached to the form.

COURSE SELECTION

An average of 300 course announcements are received by a company each month, not including course announcements contained in publications received by individuals, making it increasingly difficult to assess their relative value.

Information on regular courses by reputable organisations should be filed with that on films, programmed instruction and any other instructional aids, according to subject matter, for reference in preparing training programmes and course syllabuses.

External courses vary considerably in teaching methods, subject matter covered and depth of treatment, and criteria should be established by the company in their selection. The Carpet ITB recommends criteria be established in three categories: the firm's, the course's and the institution's providing the course. The criteria for the firm are:

1   *Orientation.* The extent to which the course must be tailored to the firm's requirements

2   *Timing and duration.* The time limit within which the course has to be available, and the amount of time the firm is willing for its nominated staff to be absent from their duties

3   *Cost.* The amount of money the firm is prepared to spend in solving the particular training need

4   *Location.* The extent, geographically, to which the firm is prepared to consider courses: local, regional, national or international

5   *Impartiality.* The extent to which the firm is prepared to consider the various types of institutions offering suitable courses

The criteria for the course are:

1   *Aims.* What the course intends to achieve

2   *Content.* What the course consists of

3   *Preparation and planning.* The care with which the course has been drawn up

4   *Staff.* The calibre of the course staff, and their suitability for the course

5   *Teaching methods.* The methods of tuition proposed and their appropriateness for the course aims

6   *Support.* The type, status and variety of students expected on the course

7   *Approval.* The extent to which the course has been approved by outside bodies

8   *Facilities.* The surroundings and physical conditions in which the course is held, for instance whether residential or non-residential

9   *Follow-up.* The extent to which the course organisers keep in touch with ex-course members in order to be of further assistance to them, or to assist in their evaluation of the effectiveness of the course

10   *Established or experimental.* Whether the course is the first of its kind, or the successor to several previous courses

11   *Qualifications.* Whether or not successful completion of the course confers any qualifications

12   *Interim liaison.* The extent to which the course organisers maintain liaison with sponsoring firms while the course is in progress

13   *Frequency.* The frequency with which the course is held

Criteria for the institution providing the course are:

1   *Success of similar courses.* How successful previous similar courses have been

2   *Emphasis on management courses.* The extent to which the institute concentrates on this type of course

3   *Standing.* The prestige of the institution

4   *Policies.* The aims of the institution
5   *Established or experimental.* Whether or not the institution is offering the courses for the first time
6   *Growth.* The measure of the expansion of the institution
7   *Government.* How the institution is governed—that is its degree of autonomy

COURSE ASSESSMENT

It is also helpful to receive reports on courses from those who have attended them, and many firms require employees to submit a report on their return from a course.

There are now two national course assessment services intended to advise companies on the selection of external courses. The best publicised is the Index of Management Courses, better known as the De La Rue Index. This service was started in 1968 by the De La Rue Company which had for some years previously been keeping assessment records of external courses for its own use. In answer to the great interest displayed by other companies in the scheme, De La Rue decided to make their information available to others on a fee-paying basis. Since then some 300 firms have subscribed.

The British Institute of Management decided to start a similar service in January 1970 but, as one of the largest course organisers in the country, it cannot hope to be as objective. And as it has not been in operation as long as De La Rue's, the BIM scheme, which in any event is limited to its members, cannot be as comprehensive.

In both schemes employees in participating companies are asked to report on courses attended and these appraisals are compiled and used to assess their comparative merits. A copy of the appraisal form, illustrated in Figure 4:3, shows the type of information used to assess courses.

In addition, course participants are asked:

1   Their objectives in attending the course
2   To what extent these were met
3   How the course content differed in any way from what had been expected, and whether or not it was appropriate to the level of delegates present on the course
4   The most useful parts of the course from a personal viewpoint
5   How these would be applied to their present job
6   What, if any, sessions they would omit and why
7   What if anything should be added to the course
8   Their opinion of the standard of instruction and individual lecturers
9   What type of person, age, position, experience and background would most benefit from the course
10   Details about the administrative arrangements, such as accommodation, timekeeping, supporting paperwork, visual aids, etc

An index of forthcoming courses is also published monthly subdivided by subject matter, and advice is given to member firms on the most appropriate available to meet individual needs.

It can happen that a manager may insist on a particular course for himself or one of his subordinates, despite adverse reports from others who have experience of it. It would seem that the training function should reserve for itself the right to decide on the most potentially valuable course for its needs. This right will not be questioned if the training function is paying the fee.

REQUESTS FOR TRAINING

Requests from individuals to attend external courses should be considered, not on the merit of the course, but on its value to the individual and to the company.

Many firms have ceased the practice of circulating course announcements within the company in the belief that individuals may be encouraged to attend courses irrelevant to their needs. Courses of unusual interest and conferences intended for senior management, however, should be sent to appropriate managers as a matter of courtesy.

In some companies requests for any kind of training must be submitted on a special form. Figure 4:4 shows the form at the British Aircraft Corporation, specifying training requirements for subordinates. Individual employees, who wish to request assistance or day release to attend a college course or evening classes, may also submit an application to the training department for approval or disapproval (see Figure 4:5).

In some other companies, requests to attend external courses are refused unless a training need has been previously established. At the Dowty Group, such requests are returned to the departmental head with an accompanying letter from the personnel director to the effect that "the single and sole criterion of courses for employees is that they be to the company's benefit" and "no doubt when you discuss this issue with him you will bear this in mind." This is usually the last that is heard of the request.

INTERNAL COURSES

In general, internal courses are more economical than external courses and are more valuable since they can be job orientated and related to the company's own operations and peculiar circumstances more easily than external courses can. External courses provide the opportunity for employees to exchange experiences with those from other companies and broaden their outlook. However they often need to be followed by internal training in any case to ensure that the acquired skill and knowledge are related to the job situation.

Internal courses also have the advantage of involving line management and specialists in training. When the expertise is not available within the company, consultants can be called in.

SCHEDULING

Having identified the type of training required it is necessary to determine the most suitable and economical arrangements for providing it.

The first step is to determine the number of courses required. This can easily be done by listing those who expressed a need for a training course according to level of course. An example is shown below.

	APPRECIATION	IN-DEPTH	ADVANCED
Work simplification	*W Lattimore* *J Hanrahan*	*J Pollard* *B Dole*	*J Galvin*
Costing	*R Bailey* *O Farmer*	*D Reilly* *J Katori*	*R Sloss* *B Maynard*

If necessary, such a list can be further divided by level of management and broad subjects, such as supervision, can be subdivided into office and shop floor supervision, for example.

COURSE SYLLABUS

A syllabus should be prepared for each course scheduled based on this information including:

1   Title of course
2   Purpose or objective of course
3   Duration
4   Dates
5   Course contents, including projects, required reading, works visits, etc
6   Training techniques (if required)
7   Previous experience or formal training required.
8   Instructors

This information is then circulated among those who are interested and those nominated to attend the course are listed on separate pages, as in the example illustrated.

Work simplification 101
1–4 April

W Lattimore, Research
J Hanrahan, Maintenance
J Pollard, Inventory
B Dole, Dispatch

It is sometimes the practice to wait until there is a suitable number to attend a course before scheduling one. This proves frustrating for employees, particularly newly-engaged people who may not be willing to wait. There are many kinds of practical ways of getting around this problem. In some firms departmental managers are held responsible for initial training which can be followed up later by a formal course. Other firms use programmed instruction, discovery learning, or projects which can be used instead of internal courses.

COURSE CONTENT

Course content should be determined by the course objectives and what the members need to know and be able to do when they are fully trained. Specific facets, such as industrial relations, should be discussed with the appropriate departmental managers. At the British Aircraft Corporation, courses are built up according to different needs; individuals simply indicate which lectures they wish to include in their own programme.

As training needs change, so must the content of the courses, naturally, and it is the responsibility of the training manager to review course contents regularly.

There are several methods for keeping abreast of changing requirements:

1   Analysis of jobs, skills and the speed required by fully trained personnel
2   Discussions with the trainees themselves
3   Performance results of former trainees
4   Discussions with departments affected by the work of departments with trainees
5   Technical journals and textbooks
6   Results of practical work completed in training

Operator training programmes are normally based on a careful analysis of the skills and tasks performed by experienced workers. This is a complex exercise; a single job can involve a dozen or as many as fifty separate tasks each of which requires analysis and a different form of training.

The degree of emphasis to be given each facet of a job in training should be determined by an objective evaluation of each task. This is done by speaking to the men working on the jobs, their superiors and anyone else closely involved, and by observation of the men actually doing the jobs.

One method, first described by a senior staff member of the Department of Employment, is to rate each task within a job description according to:

1   *Difficulty* of learning
2   *Frequency* with which the task occurs
3   *Importance* in terms of the cost of inadequate performance

Difficulty of learning. For each job a datum level of skills and knowledge is established in discussion with the people interviewed. This is normally the minimum entry qualifications/experience for the job. Interviewers are then asked to rate how difficult each task would be to learn for a man coming into the job with these qualifications/experience. The scale ranges from 3 (very difficult) to 1 (relatively easy).

Frequency. Again a three-point scale is used, with 3 meaning that, for example, the task is performed once a day; 2 meaning once a week; and 1 meaning once a month or less frequently.

Importance. In this case a rating of 3 indicates that failure to perform the task correctly could lead to danger to life or limb, for instance. A 2 indicates that such a failure could be costly and 1 indicates that a failure would result in some inconveniences.

This approach was used by MSL consultants for a study on technician training for the Gas ITB and Figure 4:6 shows a typical matrix arising from this study. A rating of 3, as will be seen, is clearly a critical task. Not only would a more detailed task analysis be required in this instance, but, when the source of difficulty has been identified, a decision to "overtrain" in the task should follow. If little or no practice in the task is obtained on the job, practice would have to be provided off the job which would allow for any decrement in performance on the job. An example of a 3-1-3 task would be crash landing for pilots; obviously training must be given off the job and refresher courses need to be given throughout a man's career.

Training need not be confined to the classroom. Related projects, games, practical exercises, works visits and planned experience are valuable parts of training and help to get trainees away from the classroom environment.

PLANNED EXPERIENCE

Planned experience in various departments, when properly organised, is useful not only in helping trainees to choose a career, but as a valuable part of a development programme. The objective of secondment should be clear and purposeful. It is helpful to provide each trainee with some kind of document listing, for instance the work in which the department is engaged, the people responsible, how departmental information is recorded and the general work flow. Many other details can be added naturally. A senior member of the department should serve as mentor. Whenever possible, the trainee should be assigned only to successful and effective teams and have specific tasks and responsibilities with the necessary feedback for the training department to be able to review his work.

A report on the work done should be written by the trainee and a copy given to training for assessment and to determine further training. The copy should then be filed in the trainee's personal folder.

PROJECT WORK

Project work is used widely, particularly for technical training and to a greater extent still for graduate and undergraduate training. The Engineering ITB among others recommends project work for technical apprentices in the various departments they work in throughout their training. Project work does not apply any longer to craft apprentices since the modular system was introduced by the Engineering ITB.

Projects should be agreed by the departmental heads in collaboration with the trainee and the training officer, and should comprise useful work, both from the training point of view and the company's.

The projects should be described in writing with a copy for the trainee, for the departmental manager, the training officer and the personal file. Joseph Lucas provides three standard forms in each trainee's programme for him to use for writing out project briefs. The form states the name and category of trainee, course, factory department, project tutor, starting and finishing dates, proposed length and work objectives (see Figure 4:7).

COURSE DURATION

There are several factors to consider in determining the duration of training:

1   Standard of performance to be achieved
2   Difficulty of subject matter
3   Capacity and capabilities of trainees
4   Cost
5   Time available

Overlong training can cause extreme boredom and consequently high labour turnover, particularly among operators who are eager to start productive work and attain higher wages. Very often, of course, training time cannot be shortened; the length of training for apprentices, for example, may be governed by a national agreement. Under other circumstances, training time can be reduced by changes in training arrangements; it can often be broken up to stimulate interest. Lessons which demand most mental concentration should be spread out. Long courses can be split into a number of modules. Perkins Engines, for instance, has seven modules for its supervisory course, each lasting two or three days, spread out throughout the year. It is also helpful to change instructors.

Apprentices at Ideal Homes Development Limited at Epsom spend their first three months in the training centre concentrating on drills in the use of tools. During the second period of six months the training officers are constantly looking for small jobs with local works departments and on building sites which require the application of newly-learned skills. When such a job is available, the instructor goes out with the apprentices, explains what has to be done and supervises it until the work is completed, inspected and accepted by the site foreman. For the final period of three months, the company tries to provide a major practical exercise.

In the last five years, five-year apprentices have built 3 two-storey four-bedroom houses with double garage, all within the cost targets set for the site. All three houses have been accepted by construction and sales departments for sale in the £12 000 price range. Initially the company felt some trepidation at undertaking a project of this size and value with trainees who had been with the company only nine months, but it decided to proceed on the basis of the evidence of the boys' ability from the many exercises which they had completed.

COURSE FACILITIES

It may be useful to draw up a checklist of details to be arranged for each course and when they must be completed, as shown in the illustration.

Work simplification 101	*April 1–7*
Book facilities	Immediately
Secure speakers	Immediately
Obtain course material	March 15
Prepare syllabus	February 15
Course announcements	March 1
Visual aids, projectionist	March 1

It is then useful to list any arrangements to be made chronologically. It may be simpler to use a separate page for each month, as shown.

	March		*Course*	*Confirmed*
1	Announce work simplification course		WS 101	
1	Book visual aids, projectionist		WS 100	
3	Announce course on work simplification		SI 36	
10	Book marketing strategy film		TM 10	Miss Pearce AB Pathe
13	Book hotel accommodation for 8 in Birmingham		SU 40	Belle Vue
Other things to do this month:				
	Check MD's secretary re: date of prize day ceremony			
	Book canteen for prize day ceremony			
	Notify wages department: Apprentices turning 18:			
		J Shaefer	12344	
		Philip Buck	67567	

Works canteens, recreation rooms and board rooms are invariably good locations to hold courses. For one reason or another, it may be preferable to hold courses away from the works. Hotels, guest houses, church halls, public houses or the local technical college may be able to provide adequate facilities. The lecture room itself should be quiet, have good ventilation, facilities for being darkened and proper electrical outlets for visual aids and amplification equipment if necessary.

Once a course is established, it can either be recorded in a diary with the relevant details or on a wall chart, as shown in the example below.

				April								May					
	24	25	26	27	28	29	30	1	2	3	4	5	6	7	8	9
Canteen		*Work Sim. 101*							*Prod. 42*							
Board room				*Marketing film:*												
Training centre								*Supervisor Crs.*								

Audio-visual aids equipment, as well as any standard course materials such as books, tools, pencil and paper required for a course, should be listed on the syllabus or noted in a diary by the person responsible. In large companies, it may be feasible to book any equipment to ensure it will be available. A set of index cards should suffice, marked as follows:

Item:				
Date needed	*Requested by*	*Location*	*Date taken*	*Date returned*

At Joseph Lucas, training officers each take weekly turns in being responsible for providing the necessary instructional material for all courses being held. A schedule is prepared for each course listing the supplies needed for each session and any other action to be taken each day. It may be necessary, for example, for the training officer to telephone a factory manager several days in advance to remind him that course members will be visiting his department that week. Everything is included in the schedule, down to carafes of water for certain individual instructors.

Printed materials are coded with the number of the course on which they are most frequently used, and filed accordingly, although it can be used on other courses. It is the responsibility of the training officer taking out material to ensure that the minimum number of copies for the next course remains. If not, he should make additional copies.

ASSIGNMENT OF TRAINEES

An individual booked to attend a course should be reminded in sufficient time to make arrangements for his absence. At the same time, he should be provided with a course programme, details of location, reporting times and of any course material he should take. If expenses are to be incurred, he should be given the authority to receive an advance from petty cash. Personnel and salary administration should be notified if the individual is scheduled to be away from the works for some length of time.

Similarly, all personnel scheduled to lecture or lead a discussion on the course should receive a copy of the programme with his session clearly indicated in some way, by a coloured label for example.

A plan is also necessary to schedule movement of trainees who need to be assigned to various functions as part of their training. There are two basic requirements: where each trainee is assigned and when he is scheduled to move. There are several methods for doing this. The methods illustrated are quite simple.

	PRODUCTION	MARKETING	FINANCE
P Dole	1–30 Jan	1–28 Feb	1–31 March
O Farmer	1–28 Feb	1–30 Jan	1–30 April
	January 1 7 14 21	February 1 7 14 21	March 1 7 14 21
P Dole	Production	Marketing	Finance
O Farmer	Marketing	Production	Stock control

These two methods have the advantage of keeping names in alphabetical order.

Scheduling is complicated if constraints are imposed on it by the number of trainees each department can accommodate at any one time. There are further complications if the length of time which each trainee needs varies from department to department or when rotation must follow a logical pattern.

The North-West London area headquarters of the Post Office uses a wall chart to govern the movement of its 250 or so telecommunication apprentices. The three-year apprenticeship scheme involves considerable on-the-job training in different types of work situations located throughout the North-West London area. The first sixteen months alone involves some fourteen different moves, none of which lasts more than six weeks. Moreover, the maximum number of apprentices each working group can take at any one time varies widely.

Initially the GPO thought of using a peg board, but before long concluded that any board which would meet their requirements would have to be huge. Their present chart covers one wall and can be expanded as the number of apprentices rises.

For their purpose North-West London has been divided into four parts, each designated by a separate colour. The same colour is then used for the cards denoting the training establishments and those bearing the names of the trainees living in the same area. In this way, at least an attempt is made to send a trainee to the training stations nearest his home.

The vertical column on the left side of the chart contains the names of every work section which can take trainees, divided by colour into four groups. Each card contains the name of the section, the jobs taught there, the instructor responsible and the maximum number of trainees that can be accommodated at any one time. To the right are vertical rows of slots. Each row represents a different week, and in each slot opposite a training section are the same number of cards as there are training places. The colour of the cards kept in this bank indicates the type of work—that is, the job to be learned by the apprentice at this section.

The first vertical column of the accompanying chart contains the names of each trainee and to the right of each name are vertical rows of slots, each row again indicating a different week. The tabs in the first chart indicating a training place are then allocated to each trainee as required. When a geographical area no longer has any tab of the required colour (indicating the job to be learned), then the trainee is allocated a place in another area. When a trainee has completed his assignment with a work section, the tab is returned to the appropriate place in the pool. Different numbers on each tab indicate to which station and to which week it belongs. On the reverse side is a number indicating the name of the instructor in charge so that at any one time the training staff not only know where an individual trainee is, but what he is learning and who his instructor is.

As the trainees are enrolled in academic courses of varying difficulty, the cards bearing the trainees' names are not listed alphabetically but in groups according to stream. This eliminates the need for filling in each slot when a group is on block release and reshuffling is minimal when one group is replaced by another on block release. White tabs refer to technical colleges, half-size tabs to local training schools and pink tabs to the Post Office's London Regional Training School at St Paul's, London EC2, Charles House, Kensington, or Kew. A colour code is used to indicate when a trainee's school report has been received and to identify which trainees have been visited personally by a training officer.

Perkins Engines use a "loading card" for planning each trainee's route for the year (see Figure 4:8). The index card has his name, grade, clock number, date of birth (for notifying salary administration of age related wage increases) and date of engagement. The left vertical column is used for listing departments to which the trainee is scheduled to be assigned and the squares opposite are filled in to indicate when he is scheduled to be there. The cards are filed alphabetically within a chronological order according to the week he is scheduled to be moved.

As a trainee is scheduled to be moved a movement form should be issued to notify the trainee and others concerned, including wages (see Figure 4:9). The movement form used at Perkins Engines (Figure 4:10) has four copies, one each for the supervising manager and the trainee, one for the "receiving" manager and the fourth is retained by the training department.

A standard form can also be used to notify the trainee himself of an impending move (see Figure 4:11).

TRAINING RECORD Part 1 Authorisation by head of department						
TO WORKS EDUCATION OFFICER						
Title of course, conference etc		Organisation		Commencing date	Finishing date	Total no of full days
Syllabus reference numbers		Location		Full time ☐	Part time ☐	
Name (capitals)	Clock number	Occupation	Dept./section	Division/works		
Authorised by Head of department		EITB group	Charge no	Fees		

Notes
1   The information on this form is used to compile a training register which the company uses to support its claim for grant from the Engineering Industry Training Board

2   It is important that this form is used to report any courses, conferences, seminars, etc, whether internal or external to be attended by any employee of the company

3   For all courses, etc, please attach a syllabus and programme

FIGURE 4 : 1   STANDARD FORM FOR REPORTING COURSE ATTENDANCE, KALAMAZOO

Analysis						Notes
Course fee	Wages or salary	Travel	Sub-sistence	Books		

FIGURE 4 : 2   RECORD OF EXTERNAL COURSES ATTENDED, KALAMAZOO

Date of entry	Employee	Details of course	Period						Number of days	Total cost			
			From			To							
			D	M	Y	D	M	Y					

FIGURE 4 : 2—*continued*

```
┌─────────────────────────────────────────────────────────────────────────────────┐
│  A  The course                                                                    │
│  Title                                                                            │
│  Run by (name of organisation running the course):                               │
│  Brief description of syllabus                                                    │
│                                                                                   │
│                                                                                   │
│  No of people present on the course                                              │
│  Principal lecturer(s)                                                            │
│                                                                                   │
│  Dates                                                                            │
│  Fees (please state whether this included cost of accommodation)                 │
│  Where was the course held                                                       │
│                                                                                   │
│                                                                                   │
│  B  The course member                                                            │
│  Name                                                                            │
│  Age                                                                             │
│  Job title                                                                       │
│  Department                                                                      │
│  Company                                                                         │
│  Location                                                                        │
└─────────────────────────────────────────────────────────────────────────────────┘
```

C Summary report (you may find it helpful to complete section *D* overleaf before giving your summary report)

Finally it would be most useful if you would summarise your opinion of the course by grading it on a 1-5 scale, ticking in the box below as appropriate

5 = Excellent
4 = Very good
3 = Good — minor points of detail could be improved
2 = Satisfactory, room for improvement
1 = weak

		1	2	3	4	5
General achievement of objectives	(a) for you personally					
	(b) for the course as a whole					
Effectiveness of the lecturers	Name					
	Name					
	Name					
	Name					
	Name					
Supporting paper-work						
Administration (timekeeping, accommodation etc)						

FIGURE 4 : 3   EXTERNAL COURSE REPORT FORM, INDEX OF MANAGEMENT
COURSES

Part I Request for training

1

Dept No/Clock No	Names	Dept/office	Job title

2   What skill/knowledge is to be acquired?   .

3   Is there a written job description for his/their jobs?   Yes/No

4   Why is the training required?

5   What pattern of course is preferred? Full-time/Day release/Evening

6   By what date should training be completed? _____

7   Request initiated by _____

Date _____

Part II Nomination for training course

Please book place(s) for the above named employee(s) on the courses indicated below

1   Organisation providing course _____

2   Course title _____

3   Location _____

4   Commencing date _____ Completion date _____

Director/manager signature _____

Designation _____ Date _____

For design budgetary control only	Course identifier
	2 4 0 0 ☐ ☐ ☐ ☐ ☐ ☐ ☐ ☐

Part III For training department use

TM	
SDO	

EITB category _____   Syllabus sighted _____

Ext course ref _____   Course booking actioned _____

Int course ref _____   Course fees actioned _____

Course identifier checked _____   Acct No and cost _____

Training department _____

Signature _____ Date _____

FIGURE 4 : 4   REQUEST FOR TRAINING, B A C

Application for assistance with day release and/or evening classes			
Age	Clock no	Department no and title	Name

Application for course

Course title and ref no. (if any)	Year or part of course	Day		College
		Day and evening		
		Evening only		

Previous study

Have you previously had day-release from this company?	Yes/No	

Exam(s) passed and subjects	(Degree, HND, HNC City & Guilds, "A" & "O" level, etc)	Date	College or school

Information required of applicant for EITB purposes

1(a) Are you a trainee attached to the training department? _____
  (b) If not, are you undergoing a programme of training devised by your department? _____

2 What is your job title?_____

3 When did you start work at this company?_____

Agreement to application from head of department or nominee	Training dept authorisation	Granted with pay	
		Granted without pay	
	Signed	Fees only	
Signed _____	Date	Refused	

Conditions

1 Course and examination fees are only recoverable through the training department general office which arranges petty cash vouchers to be signed

2 Permission for paid-release, other than on a normal college day, must be requested through the training department general office in advance in writing. Agreement to absence from work must be separately obtained from head of department/senior foreman

3 Queries relating to college attendance or studies are handled daily before 10 00 (in person through the general office, or by internal phone to extension 3028)

I have read the above notes and wish to apply for day release for the course stated.

Signed _____ (date) _____

For training department use only   EITB Category
                                                                       Folio no

FIGURE 4 : 5   APPLICATION FORM FOR ASSISTANCE WITH DAY RELEASE AND/OR EVENING CLASSES

		Task	Difficulty	Frequency	Importance
1		Diagnosis faults (pneumatic and mechanical) on control loops in production gas making plants, steam raising plants, storage tanks and pressure let down systems	3	2	2
A		Detecting elements	2	1	2
	(i)	Orific plate element	2	1	2
	(ii)	Thermocouple sheaths	2	1	2
	(iii)	Level controller	3	1	2
	(a)	mechanical	1	1	2
	(b)	pneumatic	2	2	2
	(iv)	Gas analysers	2	1	2
B		Transmitter	2	2	2
C	(i)	Recorder, or	2	2	2
	(ii)	Indicator	1	2	2
D		Controller	2	1	2
E		Trip systems	3	1	2
F		Valve positioner	1	1	2
G		Control valve motor	1	1	2

FIGURE 4 : 6   TASK ANALYSIS MATRIX, DEVISED BY M S L CONSULTANTS FOR GAS I T B

TRAINING REPORT

Name

Project number

Sheet

of

TRAINING BRIEF

Name

Factory

Category

Course

Proposed length of project

Department

Project tutor

Work objectives

Start

Finish

Training objectives

FIGURE 4 : 7   PROJECTS FORM, JOSEPH LUCAS

Name _____ Grade _____ Clock _____

Date of Birth _____ Date of commencement _____ Techn day _____

	JAN				FEB				MARCH					APRIL				MAY			
	6 10	13 17	20 24	27 31	3 7	10 14	17 21	24 28	31 4	7 11	14 18	21 25	28 2	5 9	12 16	19 23	26 30	2 6	9 13	16 20	23 27
Tool room	X	X	X	X																	
College					X	X	X	X													
Maintenance									X	X	X	X	X								

FIGURE 4 : 8   TRAINEE ASSIGNMENT CARD, PERKINS ENGINES

Transfer of Personnel

From _____ To _____ Date _____

Please note that the under-named is being transferred

Surname _____ Initials _____ Time _____ Date _____

Date of birth _____ Male/female

	From	To	Remarks
Shop/dept	_____	_____	
Clock no	_____	_____	
Occupation	_____	_____	

Rate of pay	Base £ | p	COL £ | p	Merit £ | p	Total £ | p	Base £ | p	COL £ | p	Merit £ | p	Total £ | p	

| Signature | _____ | _____ | |
| Approved | | | |

FOR THE USE OF THE PERSONNEL DEPARTMENT

_____

_____

_____

_____

Approved by

_____

Chief Personnel Officer

Note: This form to be completed and forwarded to Personnel Dept for each Change of occupation, whether within existing Dept or not.

FIGURE 4 : 9   APPRENTICE MOVEMENT ADVICE NOTE

<table>
<tr><td colspan="2" align="center">**Trainee Movement**</td></tr>
</table>

Trainee Movement

To: Current training department _____

Future training department _____

Surname _____ Forename _____

Age _____ Clock number _____ Grade _____ Date of commencement _____

Above trainee will be transferred to his future department

On _____ and remain for _____ Tech college day _____

Please ensure trainee receives attached copy

If a report card is attached this should be completed
and returned to the Training Manager before the move
takes place

FIGURE 4 : 10   TRAINEE MOVEMENT NOTIFICATION NOTE

Date _____

To: Apprentice

From: _____ (Apprentice supervisor)

You are to transfer from _____
to _____ on Monday _____
at 08 00 when you should report to Mr _____

This is important

1 This chit is to be shown to your new charge hand or foreman when you report for duty

2 If the move does not take place as arranged, or you are moved to different work by anyone other than the apprentice supervision, you are to notify the practical training office by telephone (extension 2431)

3 Please return all returnable tools to the stores before you leave the department

_____
(Apprentice Supervisor)

Please note

Owners of motor cars must
notify inspector immediately
they transfer to another department

FIGURE 4 : 11   TRAINEE MOVEMENT ADVICE NOTE

5

Assessing Training Effectiveness

Assessing training effectiveness is the heart of the matter, for if training efforts and costs are to be justified it is essential that effectiveness of training be calculated. This implies a need to maintain comprehensive and accurate records of training undertaken and performance results. It may be difficult, if not impossible, to measure training effectiveness with any degree of accuracy, but if an attempt is not made the training function is operating in a vacuum.

For training procedures to be developed properly it is essential that the company establishes whether or not:

1   Training needs were correctly identified
2   The planned training programme was adequate to meet those needs
3   The planned training was carried out
4   The various elements of training met their objectives
5   The most effective training techniques and methods were used
6   The results were commensurate with the costs
7   The same results could have been achieved more economically

The first two can be answered to a large extent by comparing training results and improvements with the original records used for assessing training needs. This may appear easier than it really is, however. It may be necessary to make more detailed investigations, through regular appraisal of performance, individual and departmental, for example. Results of such practical courses as public speaking, sales or clerical training can be easily measured, but other areas may have complicating factors which make it extremely difficult for results to be assessed.

Work journals or log books which each apprentice is required to keep by the industrial training boards will indicate whether or not he is being instructed correctly and doing the jobs according to instruction. The apprentice's comments on his work, including projects and actual production, should be inspected regularly and initialled by instructors to ensure that they are not kept on exercises longer than is required and that training is being carried out properly.

Instructors and departmental managers should be interviewed to determine any noticeable differences in employee attitudes, weaknesses in the existing training schemes, etc. One must remain suspicious, however, of claims that certain tasks were not covered. It may be that the ex-apprentice said he hadn't been taught a task when in fact he had forgotten it or, more likely, he simply dislikes this particular work. This can be easily checked on the syllabus.

USING TESTS

Test results are valuable not only in measuring comprehension and performance of trainees but in assessing the efficacy of training arrangements. Surprisingly, tests are not resented by trainees; they have a beneficial psychological effect in the sense that it gives trainees definite goals to work towards. There develops an atmosphere in which trainees feel they are working against their own standards and not against each other. From the instructor's viewpoint, tests give them an opportunity to encourage and congratulate individual trainees at the right time.

Test results and results of college examinations may be used for comparison with those of previous years, but care must be taken to avoid any false or misleading comparisons since any differences may be caused not by changes in training effectiveness but by a poorer quality of intake or more difficult knowledge or skills to be acquired.

A series of tests is used by Ideal Homes Limited to measure the progress of apprentices during training. The tests are intended to measure the skills and knowledge of each and are given after each task has been learned. The number of tests varies. At the beginning, there are many smaller tasks but they become fewer and larger as training progresses. The tests are considered as exercises and not called tests in order not to dismay boys who perform badly under trial.

At the end of each of the three periods (described in the previous chapter) comprehensive trade tests are given, incorporating exercises learned and many of the smaller tests given during that period. Test results are not recorded since each boy must eventually pass each test to continue his apprenticeship. Apprentices who fail can retake the test after four weeks. There is no limit to the number of sittings he is permitted, but he must eventually pass. Any boy incapable of making the grade would be identified by the instructor without requiring a test.

In addition, tests are given on an individual basis for any task at which a trainee is particularly good and another £0.50 a week is awarded for each test passed. These results are recorded to ensure that there is no decline in productivity or quality. If a trainee's work deteriorates during the year, the instructor has the authority to stop the bonus.

Tests are also useful for determining when training is completed. This is particularly valuable in the area of operator training where trainees are eager to go onto production and earn higher wages. At Corah Limited, new operators attend a basic one-week course in machining assembly in an off-the-job training centre. Every practice job is timed and assessed for quality and the results are recorded by the trainee herself on a standard form. This sheet is inspected regularly and checked three times a day. A daily work sheet is also completed by the trainee, giving the record time for each exercise.

Operator trainees at Corah are paid on an hourly basis until the individual's production efficiency overtakes this figure. The trainee then moves over to ordinary rates of pay. Before going on to the shop floor, an operator must have reached "experienced workers standard" as determined by wages; if she were to be earning less the line would be seriously disrupted.

All jobs done by machinists at Corah are measured in terms of time. The standard minute-type approach, that is the minute-value of work done in 1 hour, averaged over a day or week, is employed as a measure of efficiency and as a directly related measure of output. In this way, each girl's output can be evaluated and different girls on different jobs can be compared over a period of time.

On-the-job instructors, who teach basic trainees advanced and specific skills, keep records for all on-the-job training and submit them to training at regular intervals. Training keeps an alphabetical register of all operators trained throughout the year with their total performance result. These records are kept by training administration for a period of five years since a large proportion of women who leave in fact return and records are used for placement.

Each operator also keeps a quality control card, incidentally, from which inspectors take a sample survey to determine whether "booster" training is required.

POST-EXPERIENCE INTERVIEWS

Apprentices and other trainees are sometimes interviewed some months after completion of training to solicit recommendations on how training could be improved. It is not sufficient merely to solicit reactions however; favourable reactions are no assurance that the existing training arrangements are sound.

Within the Dowty Group, apprentices are interviewed formally in groups of eight or nine by the personnel director. Each one is asked what training he would have liked to have received more of, the work he is presently doing and how the training he received relates to it, whether or not it was the kind of training he had expected and how it prepared him for his present job, if he enjoys his job in terms of the responsibilities he holds, how he sees his prospects and how he feels about his training and his work generally.

Remarks are written on a standard form which is initiated for each apprentice at the completion of his apprenticeship (see Figure 5:1). Any adverse comments made by a trainee are discussed with his superior to determine the reasons for them and resolve any problems. Each ex-apprentice is then interviewed every six months until the personnel director is satisfied that he has been satisfactorily placed.

Analyses of labour turnover records may indicate high wastage in particular areas caused by poor instruction or unnecessarily long training. If so, it may be possible to reduce training time by teaching new employees the basic job content and follow this up with further training after the trainee has had experience on the job. An indication of the quality of employees who leave may be significant as they may be the best or least qualified. The relationship between the employees' rate of pay with tenure will indicate this.

PERFORMANCE APPRAISAL

Performance evaluation during and after training is probably the best method for assessing training effectiveness. Performance can be based on test results during training or through regular reports from departmental managers. Once again, however, it would be misleading to compare performance of different intakes since the academic level of each may differ considerably and bad performance may be due more to poor recruitment than a deterioration in training techniques.

A standard form is used by Bentalls Limited to request an appraisal of a trainee by a departmental head (see Figure 5:2).

Figures 5:3 and 5:4 show two different types of forms used to record assessments of the work performance, knowledge and the personal qualities of a trainee at the end of a secondment to a department. At Perkins Engines, a progress report is made to training by the departmental manager at least four times a year and the results are recorded on the trainee's personal record card. Once a year the company writes a report of a trainee's performance and progress during the year and a copy is sent to the trainee's parents.

The assessment of work performance is based on the apprentice's skill in doing his job, taking into account his effectiveness as a worker, his use of correct practices and his appreciation of safety where they apply. He is judged against apprentices in a similar category and period of training.

At the end of his period in a section or at quarterly intervals, the apprentice is questioned and an assessment is made of his knowledge of skills and techniques covered during the period. Where comprehensive lists of relevant questions exist the marking is objective and comment is restricted to how the questions were answered.

The assessment of personal qualities is based on the apprentice's attitude to his work, taking into consideration his application, initiative and potential, and are of a general nature describing the apprentice's appearance, timekeeping and conduct.

At Brush Electrical, separate forms are completed when a trainee is transferred to a different department, on his eighteenth birthday and at the end of his period in the apprentice training centre (Figure 5:5).

The cumulative results of all assessments are often recorded on a single form. Figure 5:6 shows the format used by Brush Electrical. The form used by Joseph Lucas (Figure 5:7) follows the apprentice as he moves from one department to another to inform each departmental head of his complete record of skills and assessments.

In most firms, records are normally open to apprentices if they request to see them. There are no advantages to be seen in withholding this information from them and indeed it may prove beneficial for them to see reports on them, whether or not they request it.

RATING TECHNIQUES

Some sort of rating of individual performances is sometimes considered necessary for identifying those with promotion potential, in succession planning, in considering transfers, reallocation of responsibilities and in reviewing salaries. Obviously, a manager rated as outstanding, for example, would be a likely candidate for a larger task; a very good one, probably; and an unsatisfactory one, not at all. The performance appraisal form used by the Dowty Group states the question baldly—"*Is the employee promotable?*" with the answers:

1   Immediately
2   Before long
3   Possibly
4   In due course
5   Not at all

The form for any manager recommended for immediate promotion is automatically passed to the personnel director who forthwith obtains his personal record and discusses the rating given with the reporting manager.

There are dangers in making invidious comparisons between the performance of one man and another, who may have quite different tasks to perform under very different circumstances. To be truly objective it is essential to assess a man's performance against his own goals which have been agreed, and in the light of factors influencing his success.

QUALIFICATIONS RECORDS

An inventory of human resources is as important as inventories of other company assets, and perhaps more so. The reason that companies do not carry out skills inventories more than they do is simply because of the difficulty, but more firms are becoming interested in obtaining statistics on professional and technical skills and other qualifications as personnel records are being placed on computer.

A skills inventory is invaluable to senior management in setting company objectives and in corporate planning, and we may see more and more firms making regular skills inventories as personnel records are placed on computer. A skills inventory could show, for example, the particular skills which are available and which are *not* available, before starting a project or taking on a contract. It will also indicate what recruitment and training measures must be taken to secure the missing skills.

Individual qualifications records ensure that every single employee is developed to his full capability. They are helpful in uncovering exceptional talent, in wage and salary review, for filling vacancies from within, for succession planning and establishing potential.

It must be emphasised that any inventory of manpower resources must, to be complete, include everyone and that includes what is variously called "brainpower resources" on the professional and managerial level as well as technical skills and abilities.

A qualification record card could hold any of the following details, varying according to the needs of the company:

1   Physical qualifications
2   Educational qualifications
3   Technical abilities
4   Mental qualifications
5   Merit rating
6   Social data
7   Experience
8   Progress
9   Timekeeping
10 Accident record
11 Plant activities
12 Desires and ambitions
13 Education and training
14 Transfers and promotions

The Lucas Organisation, which is placing its training records on computer, is programming its qualifications cards to derive: what an individual has done, what he should be doing and what his programme is for the future. In addition to his qualifications and achievements, the qualifications record card on computer will indicate the last type of course he attended and his potential courses. A two alpha code is used for every qualification. Each individual record carries the last two academic qualifications the employee has; when a new code is inserted, the first one falls out and the other moves up. It is also useful to record the degree of proficiency in speaking, writing or reading a foreign language.

Qualifications should be brief and concise but, above all, complete, and should be updated regularly. This can be done at the same time as staff appraisal or by initiating a form on which each individual is asked to record the qualifications he has achieved and the studies undertaken. At Perkins Engines, such forms are circulated about once every four years.

Surname	Forenames		Grade	D G category
Period of apprenticeship	Qualifications			
Occupation	Date of transfer	Date of interview	Remarks and recommendations	

FIGURE 5 : 1   EX-APPRENTICE INTERVIEW FORM, DOWTY GROUP

FROM STAFF TRAINING

To _____

May we please have a short initial report on the progress of _____
who joined your department on _____

Application of system

Any further training required
(a)   Cash register drill
(b)   System
(c)   Salesmanship

Knowledge of merchandise

Stock-keeping

Appearance

Speech

Personality

Staff training department

FIGURE 5 : 2   REQUEST FOR APPRAISAL REPORT, BENTALLS

To _____   Date _____

From _____

Confidential report on graduate/"A" level trainee

Students and trainees are always anxious to hear of their progress. I should be most grateful if you would complete the report and return it to me

1   Comment on the trainee's general contribution to the department — appearance, punctuality, etc

Strengths   Weaknesses

_____   _____
_____   _____
_____   _____
_____   _____

2   Does the trainee get on well with the other staff in the department? Is he one of the team? Does he take his full share of the work — stock-keeping, display, etc

Strengths   Weaknesses

_____   _____
_____   _____
_____   _____

3   Comment on the trainee's selling ability, attitude to customers, alertness to customers, sales compared with other staff in the department

Strengths   Weaknesses

_____   _____
_____   _____

4   How quickly did the trainee learn the range of stock, technical information about the merchandise, departmental procedures, etc

Strengths   Weaknesses

_____   _____
_____   _____

5   Comment on the trainee's knowledge of the store system. Is his/her work trouble-free?

Strengths   Weaknesses

_____   _____
_____   _____

6   How well does the trainee work independently? Does he/she find work for himself/herself? Are jobs followed through and finished off? Can he/she be relied on?

Strengths   Weaknesses

_____   _____
_____   _____
_____   _____

7   Are there any comments you would like to make that you feel would help the trainee progress?

_____
_____
_____

8   Would you be happy to have this trainee as *your* DSM at some future date?

_____

Staff training department

FIGURE 5 : 3   TRAINEE APPRAISAL FORM, BENTALLS

	Disappointing	Below average	Average	Above average	Outstanding	Remarks
Progress report						
Type	Name				Clock no.	
Period	Dept & section					
Type of work						
Aptitude						
Accuracy & finish						
Originality & resource						
Confidence & self-reliance						
Keenness & application						
Conduct						
Relations with others						

Consistent		Lively		Quiet		Dull	
Erratic		Cheerful		Grouser		Bright	
Sticker		Dour		Lazy		Careless	
Easily beaten		Talkative		Willing		Fast worker	

Supervisor comment & sign	
Head of dept, comment & sign	
Apprentice instructor comment & sign	

FIGURE 5 : 4   TRAINEE PROGRESS FORM, JOSEPH LUCAS

98

EDUCATION & TRAINING DEPARTMENT					
Completion of Apprenticeship					
Birthday Appraisal					

Name and initials				Craft apprentice,	
Department				Clock number	

Special education department instructions:

Signature education department				Date	

In respect of the 5 factors referred to below, please place a cross in the most appropriate positions

	Poor	Fair	Average	Good	Very good
1 Practical ability	Poor	Fair	Average	Good	Very good
2 Attendance in department	Poor	Fair	Average	Good	Very good
3 Initiative	Poor	Fair	Average	Good	Very good
4 Reliability	Poor	Fair	Average	Good	Very good
5 Co-operation	Poor	Fair	Average	Good	Very good

6 Details of work undertaken during this period

7 General comments

Signature _____

Department _____

This form when completed should not be given to the trainee but should be sent in a sealed envelope marked "confidential" to the education & training department

FIGURE 5 : 5   BIRTHDAY AND COMPLETION OF APPRENTICESHIP
APPRAISAL FORM

Record sheet

Name _____ Date of birth _____ Grade _____

Home address _____

Local address _____

School last attended _____

Hobbies or interests _____

Guardians full name _____

Key to columns

A	Practical ability	B	Written work	C	Reliability
D	Keenness and industry	E	Co-operation	F	Timekeeping

Key to rating

4   Very good   2   Good   0   Average   −2   Fair   −4   Poor

Week No	Department	A	B	C	D	E	F

Clock No _____

FIGURE 5 : 6   APPRENTICE ASSESSMENT RECORD SHEET, BRUSH ELECTRICAL

Stage _____ Record of training _____ Division _____

Training programme	Industrial tutor	Works department supervisor dates	Works department supervisor dates	Works department supervisor dates	Works department supervisor dates	Variations and omissions

FIGURE 5 : 7   TRAINEE ASSESSMENT FORM, JOSEPH LUCAS

6

The Economics of Training

A cost analysis of training is particularly valuable when training is first introduced and must be justified by the benefits. Proper assessment of cost can determine, for instance, whether or not a training scheme can be considered viable enough to continue. It is possible to spend more on training than can be gained from it. But assessment can determine the most economical, if not the most effective, method of training. It also indicates whether it is more economical to train on the line or maintain an off-the-job training bay, or whether to use full-time instructors or work in cooperation with others or through outside resources. It can measure the efficiency of the training administration. An instructor may well be discovered to be preparing his own visual aids when these could in fact be better prepared at half the cost by a professional illustrator.

Calculating the cost of training is neither as difficult nor as impractical as is often maintained. It is essential to single out *important* costs and *changes* in cost. It may be feasible to do occasional surveys or limit any analysis to specific areas of training, such as operator training, or on particular projects to establish their viability.

The training cost of specific schemes or apprenticeship training centres are relatively easy to calculate. The costs of training on the job are harder to calculate. One way is to determine the costs for one typical week when trainees are approximately halfway through the year's course and development. For on-the-job operator training, it may be further necessary to make a separate cost analysis for each type or group.

Unavoidable costs should as far as possible be clearly identified and separated. The training board levy itself should not be charged against training since it may encourage the training department to make efforts to recoup the cost instead of concentrating on training benefits. A number of firms record the levy as a direct labour cost, like national insurance or SET, and consider the grant as any other source of income. At least one firm charged its initial levy the first year to operating costs and has since applied any grant return to the following year's levy. In this way, only the difference needs to be accounted for each year.

Detailed procedures in calculating the costs of training fall outside the scope of this book, but they have been well covered in books written specifically on this subject. The following checklist may prove useful, however, and give an indication of the type of expenses which can be attributed to training activities:

1   Wages of instructors, office staff and trainees including overtime, commissions and bonuses
2   National insurance
3   Luncheon Vouchers or lunch subsidies
4   Pension fund contributions
5   Overheads
6   Rates
7   Maintenance and repairs
8   Security
9   Fire prevention
10   Insurance
11   Lighting
12   Heating
13   Water
14   Printing
15   Stationery
16   Telephone
17   Newspapers and periodicals
18   Furniture
19   Production materials and tools used by trainees
20   Depreciation of furniture and equipment
21   College fees
22   Books
23   Training manuals
24   Audio-visual aids
25   Travelling expenses
26   Accommodation
27   External courses
28   Consultant fees
29   Membership of professional bodies
30   Examination fees
31   Conferences and seminars
32   Prizes and awards

After an initial costing exercise, costs can be calculated according to the number of trainees or trainee days and apportioned in the same way.

QUANTIFYING BENEFITS

Basically there are four major objectives in assessing training benefits:

1   To see if the stated objectives are being met in terms of increased efficiency and productivity
2   To justify expenditure. The benefits attributable to training make it that much easier to obtain approval and funds for developing existing schemes or inaugurating new ones. Conversely, investigations may prove a training scheme to be unjustified in terms of benefits even with a grant, and that it would save money and effort for a company *not* to train—at least in one particular aspect
3   To identify areas with the most potential benefits and ensure that the right objectives are given the right priorities
4   To ensure that training being given is being implemented

This obviously requires the provision and utilisation of records for reviewing training programmes and assessing results on a regular basis. Here we list some of the possible sources of information for assessing benefits, but the details must obviously vary to suit each company:

1   Departmental reports to senior management
2   Recommendations or other proposals sent to senior management which may result in change of techniques or procedures
3   Production records
4   Plant efficiency reports
5   Quality control reports (wastage, scrap, faults, etc)
6   Dispatch and service records
7   Sales reports
8   Test results
9   Absenteeism records
10   Earnings averages

The emphasis placed on training benefits versus costs vary considerably; some feel that the results justify any expense but others need to be more cautious. The point is that management needs to be less obsessed with the levy/grant balance and place greater emphasis on the cost and rewards instead.

An ITB grant is intended to meet a substantial proportion of a company's training expenses, but generally a company cannot determine the grant it will receive in advance, even when the board's recommendations are followed to the letter. A grant has no relation to the levy paid and, in some areas, depends more on the administration of a training board than the quantity or quality of training carried out in a firm. If anything, it is the difference between the levy and the grant that should matter to a company.

If the grant received is less than the levy paid then this may be considered the price for *not* training and can only be compared logically with the cost of implementing the ITB's recommendations *and the benefits to be derived*. If a grant is greater than the levy, then the difference may be regarded as a reward to be added to the other benefits.

CONTROL SYSTEMS

The availability of such data implies the provision of controls which can act as links and provide the necessary information. There are three essential activities involved in control:

1   Investigation of actual performance
2   Comparison of actual performance with planned performance and the establishment of any variance
3   Initiating action to cope with the observed deviation

The Lucas system of controls

The common basic information to be found in each company within the Joseph Lucas Organisation includes:

> Factory budget
> Operating summary
> Manufacturing data sheet
> Departmental weekly rating sheet

The only type of information fundamental to all Lucas companies and in all functions is in the area of budgeted labour figures and overhead expenditure, where targets are set and control information supplied regularly. Control information is normally geared to data processing in all areas except production.

By far, financial control is the most useful and most suitable factor of control primarily because it is easily understood and because it ultimately indicates company success or failure. There are three forms of financial control with the Joseph Lucas Group:

1   *Historical control.* This compares past performance with present performance, future action being determined by the trend disclosed by the information
2   *Current control.* This is the control used on an *ad hoc* basis day to day and is characterised by such action as the build-up or run-down of stocks without consideration of future requirements
3   *Budgetary control.* This is the most positive type of control since it involves the continuous comparison of the actual financial situation with the budgeted one and provides the explanation of any divergence

There are three other forms of controls used at Lucas:

1   *Quality control.* This indicates the degree of achievement of standards, and also forms part of the adjusting mechanism that must exist so that processes can be kept under control
2   *Programme control.* This is designed to highlight those activities, projects and so on which are not progressing at the correct rate. Critical path networks are often used as a means of planning and controlling a complex work programme. Gantt charts and bar charts are used in a similar way in connection with training benefits
3   *Quantity control.* This is concerned with controlling the amounts of stock of parts and material held in the company, or the total quantity to be produced

The following checklist provides some of the quantifiable benefits arising from close control of the training activity:

1   Reduction in accidents
2   Reduction in scrap or waste
3   Reduction in operating costs
4   Increased productivity
5   Reduction in warranty claims through improved quality
6   Increased sales
7   Reduction in idle time
8   Improved customer service
9   Reduced capital investment in stock
10   Reduction in recruitment and turnover costs
11   Increased levels of efficiency

It is important, however, to assess just how much of any improvement or change in conditions can be directly related to training effectiveness and how much was brought about through other contributing factors, such as new equipment, increased supervision or new payment methods.

One must also include work produced by trainees and by ex-trainees who have achieved the standards of experienced workers in a shorter time through improved training methods. The avoidance of labour turnover costs is a substantial benefit, but, in a positive sense, the gains from the retention of skilled labour are readily measurable.

A recent study showed that increased production from improved performance was worth only about a third of the benefits of increased production achieved through retention of skilled labour, even considering the higher wages and increased bonuses. In fact, Professor Brinley Thomas of University College, Cardiff, found that benefits due to retaining skill accrue almost entirely to the firm.

A number of methods to compute improvement in output and reduction in labour turnover were tried but the simplest and most accurate method he found was to total the output of the members of each intake of trainees in the year and divide it by the average length of stay. The average total output produced by each individual is measured in minute value of work done and the production situation at the end of each year is compared for various intakes.

INTANGIBLE BENEFITS

Training benefits cannot be evaluated in terms of money alone, however. Management must also consider other benefits which are often ignored simply because of the difficulties in measuring or evaluating them. But they, in fact, prove to be far more significant:

1   Increased adaptability of employees
2   Fewer demarcations of labour
3   Greater individual job satisfaction
4   Improved communications
5   Better capital investment decisions
6   Greater acceptance of training and of the need for retraining
7   Smaller number of grievances
8   Improved company image and consequent increase in sales and improved recruitment. The technical competence of sales staff and availability of trained maintenance and service staff are bound to be important factors in a company's marketing strategy

Any inventory of training benefits become valueless, however, unless management is satisfied that the quantity and quality of personnel provided could not be obtained in any other way.

For this reason the Dowty Group maintain a chart of all those who have been trained, including their qualifications, and plot their development to indicate how far they have gone. The group considers the number of apprentices in senior management and the proportion of executives and senior directors who have been promoted from within as fair indications of how well the company-trained staff are considered and ultimately just how valuable training is.

In the end, no doubt, the finest assessment can be made in a simple visual examination of what it would cost the company *not* to train. As basic as that. One company which **tried** this asked itself the question: "Where would we be if we did not have training?"

The answer was brief and overwhelming: the company would long ago have gone out of business.

INDEX

Index